# NDEBELE

## A PEOPLE & THEIR ART

# NDEBELE
## A PEOPLE & THEIR ART

AUTHOR: IVOR POWELL
PHOTOGRAPHER: MARK LEWIS
NDEBELE ADVISOR & PROJECT CO-ORDINATOR: MARK HURWITZ

**Struik Publishers (Pty) Ltd**
(a member of the Struik Publishing Group (Pty) Ltd)
Cornelis Struik House, 80 McKenzie Street
Cape Town 8001

Reg. No. 54/00965/07

The publishers wish to acknowledge, with thanks,
permission granted by the individuals and institutions
listed below to reproduce their photographs. Copyright
for the photographs rests with the photographers/
institutions and/or their appointed agents.

• **BMW of North America Inc./Bill Fitzpatrick Photo-
graphy**: pp 151; 153 (bottom left and right); back cover (top)
• **G Cubitt**: 77; 101 • **A Elliot**: 17; 108; 127 (left) •
**W Knirr**: 52 (left); 53-55; 58-59; 76 • **D Hemp** (Struik
Image Library): pp 114 (far right); 115 (top left and right);
122 (top right, bottom); 123 (top); 124 (top right) •
**McGregor Museum**, Kimberley, for photographs from the
Duggan-Cronin collection: pp 12-15; 20-22 • **Museum
Africa**: pp 18; 23-25; 38 • **N Knight and S Priebatsch**,
*Ndebele Images*, 1983: pp 155 (bottom left, from the
McGregor Museum's Duggan-Cronin collection); 155 (bot-
tom right); 156 (top left) • **H Potgieter**: 56-57; back cover
(middle left) • **W Raats** (copyright owner)/**John Oliver**
(photographer): 114 (bottom); 131 (left); back cover (middle
right) • **Smirnoff**: 152-153 (top). Photographer T Meintjies.
Artwork G Davis, Advertising agency Tholet and Sievers and
Association • **The Read Contemporary Gallery**: pp 143
(top); 148 (top); back cover (bottom)

**Managing editor:** Valerie Streak
**Assistant editor:** Pippa Parker
**Publishing manager:** Annlerie van Rooyen
**Design and cover design:** Alix Gracie
**Design director:** Janice Evans
**Cartographer and illustrator:** Steven Felmore

Reproduction by Hirt & Carter (Pty) Ltd, Cape Town
Printing and binding by Tien Wah Press (Pte) Ltd,
Singapore

ISBN 1-86825-691-X

# CONTENTS

# PREFACE

ABOVE: *A detail from the walls of the homestead of Francina Ndimande, one of the foremost exponents of the art of Ndebele wallpainting. The black-and-white designs in the upper section of the frame have a long history; the coloured designs in the bottom two-thirds are distinctively modern.*

We knew from the start that we were not going to find the kind of Africa that coffee table books usually favour: pristine tribal Africa – Africa still there to be seen and savoured in ways that defy the passage of three hundred years of history – Africa in all its strangeness and glory, miraculously unaffected by its colonial and post-colonial past. After all, as a collector of Ndebele art and artefacts, project co-ordinator Mark Hurwitz had been travelling in the area long enough to know that the inexorable process of history and change were taking over.

We also knew that much of the material culture commonly identified as 'traditionally' Ndebele had a far shorter history than the word 'traditional' implies. None of the beadwork made prior to the 1880s has survived, and in fact nearly all of the so-called 'characteristic' styles and designs of Ndebele art have emerged since the 1920s. The history of the colourful geometric wall-painting of the Ndebele is even shorter, the first examples dating from the late 1940s.

Of course, the roots of Ndebele culture and the belief structures that condition it extend back into a time long before whites penetrated the hinterland of southern Africa. But this fact notwithstanding, the culture that we would identify today as distinctively Ndebele is, however ironically, one which came into being during colonial and post-colonial times, and in many important ways bears the imprint of, responds to, and has been conditioned by the dominant culture of the whites.

This interpretation of Ndebele art and culture – of it having one foot in the African past and the other in the historical present – is one that, throughout, has underwritten our approach to the subject matter. It is somewhere between the indigenously African and the historically adaptive that we have looked to find the meanings and significances of Ndebele material culture. Hence we – and particularly photographer Mark Lewis – have taken a somewhat different approach to that usually pursued in books on the subject of Ndebele art.

Most writers on the subject have tended to stress the proliferation of beadworking and wallpainting after the 1940s as a powerful assertion of an African identity in defiance of the encroachments of Western civilization, and thus to emphasize the exoticism of Ndebele art. While not disagreeing with the basic argument that much of what is distinctively Ndebele is a reaction against attempts on the part of successive governments to break the power constituted by the tribal identity of the Ndebele, our approach has been far more ambivalent. It has appeared of significance to us – as indeed it did to researchers Betty Schneider and Diane Levy, among others – that Ndebele wallpainting should have flourished particularly under the spotlight of tourist attention, and equally, that Ndebele beadwork has been a tradable commodity for decades. Equally, it has seemed significant to us that the emergence of Ndebele wallpainting styles should have been actively assisted and promoted by the National Party government in pursuance of its policies of ethnic separatism.

In short, where many books on the subject would want to find some kind of spiritual purity in the art of the Ndebele, we have been conscious of the host of contradictory impulses that came together to create the often splendiferous and always fascinating corpus of Ndebele art – some of them noble, some venal, others as internally ambivalent as life itself.

Our interpretation of Ndebele art and culture has diverged in varying degrees from those of other researchers – in Mark Lewis' photographs and in Mark Hurwitz's logistical selection and emphasis, as much as in my text. Nevertheless, our debt – and mine as the writer in particular – to those who researched the Ndebele people before us remains enormous. I would mention in particular the following people and their works: the groundbreaking work of Wits University historian, Peter Delius, on the tribulations of the Ndzundza, a branch of the Ndebele in the late nineteenth and early twentieth centuries; Diane Levy's MA thesis on Ndebele beadwork; Elizabeth Schneider's PhD thesis on the wallpainting of the Ndebele; the work of Professor W D Hammond-Tooke on traditional healing in Africa; and Peter Rich's MA thesis on the meanings of Ndebele architecture.

While all of these sources, and a number of others (all written during the 1980s) were freely used, the irony is that the world we found was so changed that, for the most part, the relevance of those sources was in determining the way things used to be. Now, only a few short years later, the culture has lost its old clarities of purpose and moved into more ambiguous spaces. In the end it is to the Ndebele people and their unfailing humour and candour that we owe our greatest debt. It would be churlish to single any out, but most of these are covered by recording our indebtedness to all the Mahlangus, the Skosanas, the Mtswenis, the Ndimandes, the Ndalas, the Masombukas and the Ntulis which we encountered in our travels.

Beyond these we would like to record our thanks to our interpreters and guides: Lettie Skosana, without whose knowledge of KwaNdebele this project could quite literally not have been completed; and to Bushy Adam Mokwena who, though himself of Xhosa extraction, shared his knowledge of Ndebele custom and tradition in ways that deeply enriched our understanding of a great many issues.

We were greatly assisted in preparing the book by the Standard Bank Collection of African Art, housed at the University of the Witwatersrand Art Gallery, whose administrators allowed us access to the collection for purposes of photographic documentation; also by Citylab Professional Photo Lab, who not only performed work of the highest quality but who generously did so at a considerable discount.

Thanks also are due to Rayda Becker, curator of the Gertrude Posel Gallery at the University of the Witwatersrand, for her unfailing helpfulness in every progressively bizarre request we brought to her door. Special thanks must come from the author to Rayda for serving as a sounding board throughout the tortuous process of writing the text.

## A NOTE ON THE TEXT

Like many African languages, Ndebele is still in the process of being standardized as a written language, and the various dialects that are actually spoken do not necessarily conform with the rules that the grammarians are putting in place. This is particularly true in the case of the

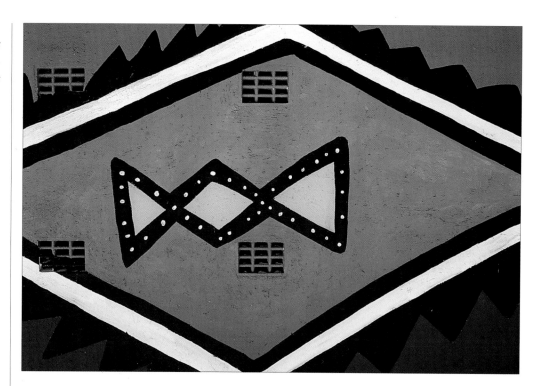

names given to such things as items of beadwork, where the commonly used words are often not the academically sanctioned ones; in many cases they have been transcribed in the first instance by non-Ndebele-speaking researchers, and differ substantially from those sanctioned by the language experts.

Nevertheless, such terms remain in common use, and so do the bastardized plurals ascribed to them in much of the material written about the Ndebele and their art. This poses serious difficulties for researchers. Does one adopt the academically correct version at the expense of familiarity? Or, does one go with the more commonly used word? The decision that I have taken is to register the existence of both usages, using whichever version seemed more appropriate in the context, relying on the reader to consult the glossary – where variants are listed – should confusions arise. For the record, the prefix 'isi' indicates a singular, while 'izi', and 'ama', indicate plural forms.

I have adopted a similarly eclectic approach to more general but similarly fraught and academically knotty issues. To take one example, the word 'tribe' does not reflect a specifically African reality, but rather one imposed by the colonials. I have used it, as I have used similarly contentious terms, without apology: partly for convenience in a book aimed at the general reader, partly because the alternatives are so cumbersome, partly because the imprint of colonists has been sufficiently strong to meaningfully imbue such notions with reality.

ABOVE: *Decorative details from Ndebele walls. It is relatively modern in design, dating from the mid to later 1980s; in it there is to be read a move away from the definitively 'Ndebele' designs of earlier decades and towards a more generic and less distinctive kind of decoration.*

INTRODUCTION

# THE ANXIETY OF THE ANCESTORS

*The idea of African society as being static and somehow outside of history is a myth
nurtured by the West. Ndebele culture, like any other, adapts to and looks to interpret changing
circumstances. As we watch, circumstances are changing so radically that it may be
adapting itself right out of distinctive existence.*

There is a passage from the distinguished anthropologist Claude Levi-Strauss's *Triste Tropique* which has always moved me and seemed to penetrate decisively the psychology underlying our approach to those societies that, until recently, we were pleased to refer to as primitive or undeveloped. Levi-Strauss writes:

Our great western civilisation, which has created the marvels we now enjoy, has only succeeded in producing them at the cost of corresponding ills... . So I can understand the mad passion for travel books and their deceptiveness. They create an illusion of something which no longer exists but should exist, if we were to have any hope of avoiding the overwhelming conclusion that the history of the past twenty thousand years is irrevocable... . There is nothing to be done about it now... .

Part of Levi-Strauss's argument is that the way we understand tribal cultures says more about 'us' (those partaking in the Western sense of history) than it does about the people it is representing. In its path to world domination the civilization of the West has wreaked enormous devastation and provoked universal spiritual and societal transformation. Rather than face up to the responsibility of such global engineering, the civilization, at basically unconscious levels, prefers to offer up to itself the illusion that differences still persist, that the clock can be turned back, that the exotic orchids of remote cultures still bloom, that the precolonial condition has not been lost forever.

There is of course a lot more to the question than just this. The rendering of alien cultures as being 'backward' justifies the West in its useful belief that imposing its own values equates with 'progress'. In similar vein, by denying history and development within the cultural usages of other peoples, the West has suppressed the fact of the historical disjunctions it has wrought, the psychic violence for which it is historically responsible.

African tribal cultures, like any others, have always been dynamic, responding to and incorporating historical events as much as natural cataclysms and human interactions. Like all forms of knowledge, all world views and mythologies, African tribal usages are in the end a means to understanding, ordering and controlling the world. Events of overwhelming significance will be appropriated within the overriding belief structure, interpreted in terms of its

assumptions, brought into line with the ever expanding body of lore that informs the life of the society and finds articulation in its ritual and material culture. If, however, transformation, adaptation and change represent one pole of the way that knowledge functions in tribal societies, the other is that of continuity. This end of Ndebele life is especially expressed in their worship of the ancestors, or honoured dead of the tribe. It is the ancestors particularly who demand that tradition be maintained, the old customs be observed and the special identity of the group be reaffirmed. Thus, broadly considered, the culture of the tribe is in a constant state of flux, pushed on by history, pulled back by jealous ancestors, and in this way a balance is maintained.

But now, in the 1990s, this characteristic balance is in jeopardy. The precariousness of the cultural moment is particularly poignantly noted in the fact that though the majority of rural Ndebele continue to make some form of 'traditional' beadwork, it is stylistically so changed that it no longer possesses any ritual efficacy; the ancestors, so older informants told us, neither recognize nor acknowledge the so-called 'party-style' appurtenances.

Even the founding observances of the society are in danger. Many youths nowadays run away rather than endure the male initiation – involving as it does circumcision by penknife and three months of seclusion in the mountains. Others check in at hospitals to have the foreskin surgically removed. Even so, each time the initiation is performed – which in South Africa is every four years, and by all the southern African Nguni tribes excepting the Zulus – dozens of youths die, and the practice has increasingly come under attack from health authorities and the black intelligentsia. The question, as the twenty-first century looms, is whether the ancestors themselves are going to survive. In truth, without that self-replenishing, endlessly authoritative pool of the Ndebele dead, the culture cannot sustain itself, except perhaps as a commercial tourist diversion. With the spread of Western education and, perhaps most significantly, the ascent to government in 1994 of the essentially non-tribal African National Congress, the ancestors are under siege. And their existence grows more and more anxious as the younger generation moves into the cities, abandoning old customs and buying into the postcolonial world. It will not happen overnight, but it is hard to avoid the conclusion that the pole of continuity represented by the ancestors is losing out to that of change, and the tribal culture gradually adapting itself out of existence.

PIETERSBURG

STRYDPOORTBERGE

DRAKENSBERG

Potgietersrus

Olifants

Ohrigstad

Groblersdal

Steelpoort

Dennilton

Lydenburg

Weltevrede Farm

Roossenekal

David Mahlangu

Wallmansthal

Doornkop

Stoffberg

PRETORIA

Hartebeesfontein Farm

Botshabelo

Bronkhorstspruit

Middelburg

JOHANNESBURG

Springs

Devon

Morotse

Mahlangu Area

Motetema

Steelpoort

Groblersdal

KoNomtjharhelo

Kgono

Blood

Buffelsvallei

Rooikraal

Kafferskraal

Brakfontein

# CHAPTER 1
# THE HISTORY OF THE NDEBELE

*Emerging as a strong regional force in the wake of the great southern African upheavals of the early
19th century, the Ndzundza Ndebele were finally defeated by the whites of the Transvaal Republic in 1883,
and virtually enslaved. But this catastrophe – and those which were to follow under generations of white rule
and apartheid – served merely to strengthen cultural ties and their expression in art.*

ABOVE: *One of Alfred Duggan-Cronin's photographs taken in the Wallmansthal area in the 1930s. The architecture reflects a Sotho influence. The floor markings recall the 'tyre tracks' which are often found on Ndebele walls.*
OPPOSITE: *An Ndebele woman and child from Duggan-Cronin's portfolio, taken among the Manala Ndebele in the Wallmansthal area in the 1930s. Note the* golwani *around the neck and* dzilla *on the legs. The flimsiness of these appurtenances compared with those found among the Ndzundza Ndebele today, is often taken to distinguish the two branches, but the distinction is not universally observed.*

We know very little about the why and the how, but there is evidence that sometime (by Western chronology) in the third or fourth century AD the forefathers of the present Nguni tribes had reached Mozambique and northern Natal. These people were members of the Bantu language and cultural group and had migrated in a southeasterly direction from earlier habitats in Central and West Africa.

From this base the Southern Nguni, along with their Bantu cousins, the Sotho-Tswana (who had moved southwards to the region primarily along the west coast), gradually settled the southern African subcontinent. As they did, so they came into contact with one another and probably with various other peoples already in the area. In the process the original culture was transformed: intermarriage, cultural borrowings and assimilations resulted in a variety of hybridizations and the emergence of a range of different identities and groupings within both the Sotho-Tswana and the Nguni strains. Eventually, in the case of the South Nguni stock, the new groupings would be identifiable as the Zulu, Xhosa, Swazi and Ndebele groups we recognize today.

By the 16th century AD, the Ndebele had acquired a more or less separate identity – a proto-version of the group we know today, though not in all respects identical: major upheavals were to follow in the 19th century; further processes of cultural and political cross-fertilization. The Ndebele by this time had also split into Northern and Southern branches, though the Northern branch, as a result of assimilation with the Sotho-Tswana, has all but disappeared today. (This Northern Ndebele branch should not be confused with the Matabele of Zimbabwe, followers of the Zulu warlord Mzilikazi, who are also, and confusingly, referred to as Ndebele.)

Exactly what circumstances brought about the various fragmentations and transformations of the original Nguni stock remains unclear. Some light may be cast on the subject by oral historians, however. King Mayisha II (also known as Cornelius), reigning monarch of the dominant Ndzundza branch of the Southern Ndebele, explained the emergence of the Ndebele nation as follows:

The Ndebele are part of the Zulus, and what happened there was that they parted from the Zulus and they came all the way to the Transvaal. The Ndebele first came from Pietermaritzburg. They were a nation there which was still part of the Zulus. They had many cattle and much wealth. Then Shaka began to feel very much inferior. And he said: 'Hey, part of my people they are down there and they have more cattle than I have.' So he sent down his advisors to call down that chief to come and talk to him. But the captain when he comes there he tells them: 'Hey, you'd better look out. Be careful, you are going to be destroyed because Shaka wants part of your cattle.' So these people decided 'No, we're not going there. We are not going back, we are going forward.'

So they took all their cattle and their possessions and they went forward. So while they were heading forward, they parted from the others. Some went the other side to Swaziland. Those were the people who said they fight nobody, those are the people who just want to stay in peace.

Then our people with Mzilikazi and Mshobani went down, and they started to have all this fighting. Then they came to the caves and they stayed there at Roossenekal. Then some people went behind the mountain and they called themselves Pedi, then some people went further and they called themselves Matabele — those were Mzilikazi's people, who went past Beit Bridge into Zimbabwe...).

In literal terms, King Cornelius' version is flawed to say the least. Half of the story he is telling is that of his own people; the other half is that of the Matabele, who under Mzilikazi — half brother and rival of the great imperialist Zulu king, Shaka — broke away from the Zulu polity in the 1820s to spearhead a wave of Zulu aggression. This destructive campaign, along with the violence wrought by the white colonists as they cut a parallel swathe through the subcontinent, led to the Difaqane (or Mfecane) — 'the scattering of the people'. At this time the Southern Ndebele (King Cornelius' people) had been established

in what later became the Transvaal for at least three centuries, and in fact the only real contact they had with Mzilikazi was in combat during his aggressive advance.

Nonetheless, there is probably some truth to be extracted from King Cornelius' chronicle: that of a migration or a series of migrations from present-day KwaZulu/Natal, into the hinterland. The evidence of language and custom suggests that the early Nguni immigrants did in fact move down along the east coast to present-day KwaZulu/Natal, and that from there migrations took place which led to the emergence of the Swazi and Ndebele peoples. And, while the Pedi are not strictly a people, but a collection of disparate societies bound together on political and military levels, it is true that some of the elements which went into that cultural melting pot were of Nguni origin.

Thus, despite the confusions and the weavings together of remembered fact with folklore and fiction in King Cornelius' version, he is probably right in suggesting a series of migrations during the (Western) Middle Ages out of present-day KwaZulu/Natal and into the hinterland. There may even be some truth in his explanation as to why the Ndebele migration took place: the Nguni king was jealous of the wealth in terms of cattle belonging to one of his vassal chiefs and demanded they be handed over; whereupon the subject chief refused, choosing to flee with his followers rather than face the alternative of war. As for the Ndebele themselves, once in the region later

BELOW: *Sangomas in the 1930s; the word 'sangoma' means 'person of the drum'.*
BOTTOM RIGHT: *Prints such as that worn by the woman here are so common throughout Africa as to seem almost indigenous. In fact, they are imported — in the past from the UK, nowadays from the East. Interestingly, such prints are seldom worn by the Ndebele today.*

known as the Transvaal, they also fragmented – by their own genealogical accounts 10 generations of kings ago, and according to modern historians around the end of the eighteenth century. Apparently, the cause was some kind of struggle for succession. According to Ndebele oral history, the split came about when Ndzundza, a younger son of King Msi, cheated his elder brother Manala (the rightful heir) out of the chieftainship in a story that echoes powerfully that of Esau and Jacob of the Old Testament. As a result, the kingdom was divided, so the story goes, among five brothers, giving rise to the Ndzundza and Manala branches of the tribe, though no record exists of what happened to the other three subgroups.

Whatever the truth of the story or its dating, the Southern Ndebele of today continue to fall into two subgroups: the Ndzundza, who have traditionally been ruled by the lineage of King Cornelius, and the Manala.

Severely decimated in the ravages of Mzilikazi, the Manala eventually found their way (by the 1930s) to Wallmansthal, near Pretoria. At that time, according to such researchers as the government ethnologist N J van Warmelo, the Manala were reported to be important producers of beadwork, but since then this group has ceased to nurture any very significant material traditions and it never became involved in the explosion of wallpainting that occurred in the 1940s and the years that followed.)

But why should the culture of the Ndzundza have flourished while that of the Manala gradually disappeared? There is no definitive answer to the question. Still, one might venture a seemingly perverse speculation: that the culture of the Manala failed to survive precisely because, unlike the Ndzundza, they were not persecuted as a group. Unlike the Ndzundza, the Manala were not forced by special historical circumstances to stick together, and thus, like the vast majority of South African blacks, became increasingly detribalized the more they were subject to processes of urbanization. Today, although there is a Manala initiation held in the Steelpoort district, there is little else that sets the culture of the Manala apart from that of their neighbours in the townships. Indeed, the

ABOVE: *An Ndebele settlement in the earlier part of the century. Note the central enclosure in which all of the village's cattle would have been housed at night.*

CHIEF NYABELA 1883

THIS MONUMENT IS ERECTED AND

OPENED ON 19·12·70.

BY PARAMOUNT DAVID MAPOCH

ON BEHALF OF THE NDEBELE

NATION TO EXTEND PEACE

GOODWILL AND UNITY TOWARDS

ALL NATIONS.

National Party authorities had to all but manufacture a chieftaincy among the Manala when, in the 1950s and 1960s, they set up networks of tribal authority in pursuit of their policies of ethnic separatism.

The Ndzundza, by contrast, survived as Ndzundza and the reasons are, at least in part, inscribed in their history. Around 1840 a king by the name of Mabhogo ascended to the Ndzundza monarchy, which had practically been destroyed in the conflicts of the early 19th century. Gathering his straggling followers about him, Mabhogo undertook a further migration in search of some fortress where his people could defend themselves.

He found such a fortress near present-day Roossenekal at a spot the Ndebele call KoNomtjharhelo, but which is more familiarly known today as Mapoch's Caves. The stronghold of KoNomtjharhelo lies in the hill country east of Roossenekal. It is found at the top of a long, steep climb through dense tangles of tropical undergrowth topped by long fingers of tree-cactus that grow from vast trunks often worthy of baobab trees. It is a place of rugged outcrops and dramatic ravines, of strange, twisting vegetation and deep silences; an alien place, forbidding in atmosphere and difficult in access even at the best of times. Beneath this harsh crust of earth there is a complex and secret network of natural caves, which – at least to nineteenth century technology – rendered the place virtually impregnable against attack.

Thus fortified against their would-be enemies, and occupying some of the richest farmland in South Africa, the Ndzundza Ndebele prospered until the end of the 1870s. During this time, the fortress kingdom attracted significant numbers of refugees from other communities that had survived the Difaqane – particularly Sotho-speakers – and these refugees grafted much of their own tradition on to the Nguni culture of the Ndzundza.

This hybrid community grew very quickly into a force powerful enough to repulse the armies of the Boers of the Zuid Afrikaanse Republiek (ZAR) in 1849 and again in 1863, as well as a powerful Swazi army in 1864. By the next decade, although they numbered scarcely more than 10 000 in total, they constituted one of the most powerful tribal groupings in the northern half of South Africa. But towards the end of the 1870s, 'behind the mountain' among the Pedi in Sekhukuneland, the seeds of destruction were being sown.

Prior to the reign of Mabhogo and the emergence of a specifically Ndzundza power, the Ndzundza Ndebele had been merely one of the vassals within an influential Pedi power bloc, paying subservient tributes and providing the Pedi king, Sekhwati, with regiments in times of war.

However, with the increase in Ndzundza influence after their remove to Mapoch's Caves, such obeisances had lapsed, and in 1861 with the accession to the Pedi paramount chieftaincy of King Sekhwati's eldest son, Sekhukune, conflict between the two groupings became increasingly open.

Failure to pay tributes to Sekhukune was only one of the reasons for tensions between the Pedi and the Ndzundza. The other was rooted in a bitter dispute over Pedi succession between Sekhukune and his younger half-brother, Mampuru. Though not in line for succession, it was Mampuru who had been designated by the dying Sekhwati to succeed him as king. However, when the old king died, Sekhukune moved swiftly to assert his right of succession and have himself ceremonially installed, leaving Mampuru out in the cold. Not unexpectedly, Sekhukune's coup led to the Pedi, and equally their vassals, splitting into two factions and was the source of the bitter feuding which dragged out over more than 20 years. In the Pedi civil conflict, the Ndzundza found themselves on the side of Mampuru.

Finally, in 1882, the conflict reached crisis point when about 30 of Mampuru's men attacked the kraal of Sekhukune and slew the elder brother. However, until his death, Sekhukune had dealt favourably with the Boers of the ZAR, allowing them to settle in areas under his control, and on more than one occasion he had even joined forces with the Boers in military campaigns against common enemies. Though dealings with Sekhukune had always been uneasy, they were nevertheless of vital importance to the Boers. With Sekhukune dead and Mampuru, who had always been bitterly opposed to white settlement, in a position to consolidate the Pedi monarchy against them, the Boers set about hunting Mampuru down. Mampuru, meanwhile, had sought refuge with one of the sub-chiefs of the Ndzundza and thus – in accordance with tribal etiquette – became the ward of Nyabela, reigning Ndzundza regent at the time. Nyabela consistently refused to betray his Pedi ally. To have done so, explained no less an authority on Ndzundza etiquette than King Cornelius (reigning monarch of the Ndzundza today), would have constituted an unthinkable breach of tribal honour.

Whatever the reason for this decision, Nyabela's intractability made the Boers importunate. Having first tried to bribe the Ndzundza regent with 200 head of cattle in exchange for the Pedi pretender, they progressed swiftly to threats and then finally to a proclamation of state in October 1882, whereby Commandant General Piet Joubert was authorized to use whatever means might prove necessary to apprehend Mampuru.

Nyabela's response, duly recorded by history, was as colourful as it was ominous. He had swallowed Mampuru, he told the Boers, and if they wanted the Pedi prince, they would have to cut him (Nyabela) open.

On 7 November 1882, months of standoff finally culminated in the formal declaration of war by the ZAR. Though it hardly needed an excuse, one was given when Nyabela's men, under cover of darkness, descended on Joubert's commandos, who were encamped on the plains below Mapoch's Caves in readiness for confrontation, and returned to the caves with a significant number of the cattle the Boers had brought along for supplies.

The Boers had no easy time of it. The Ndzundza were armed with guns, and every attack launched by Joubert's men on the main fortifications was easily repulsed. On more than one occasion the Boers found themselves led into cunningly constructed ambushes amid the network of caves, military fortifications and blind alleys that made up the mountain fortress. Finally, Joubert changed tactics and lay seige to the fortress, cutting off supplies from the outside. At the same time, his men, unable to gain access to the fortified heart of the caves, attacked peripheral sections of the fortress, particularly those where crops were grown and livestock kept. Using dynamite, they destroyed many of the Ndzundza's storage areas. In this way Joubert slowly starved the Ndzundza out.

It took eight months before Joubert's tactics bore fruit. Slowly starving, the Ndzundza were forced to surrender, and a chief was despatched by Nyabela to surrender the handcuffed Mampuru to the Boers.

With the mighty Ndzundza at their mercy, the Boers of the ZAR were not content merely with Mampuru. The Ndzundza royal kraal was razed and its cattle seized. Nyabela himself was arrested and sentenced to death – though, following the intercession of the British, the punishment was later commuted to life imprisonment with hard labour (in chains). Mampuru was not so lucky; he was hanged in late 1883.

This was only the beginning of the ZAR's revenge. In the aftermath of the war, the ZAR parliament declared the Ndzundza their conquered subjects. Next, they solemnly estimated the costs of the war to be nearly £50 000, compensation for which was exacted in two ways. In August 1883 all the lands of the Ndzundza – some 36 000 hectares – were confiscated and divided mainly among the Boers who had fought Nyabela. In addition, a ban was placed on 'all kaffer kraals or tribes large or small' on that land. Not considering this enough – and wanting, above all, to prevent the Ndzundza from ever consolidating their power again – the ZAR parliament also declared that the

OPPOSITE: *The statue of the warrior Nyabela at Mapoch's Caves.*
BELOW: *On 19 December each year, the faithful traditionalists among the Ndzundza Ndebele gather at Mapoch's Caves to assert the culture the Boers thought they had broken after the defeat of the Ndzundza Ndebele there in 1883. The two old men in the picture are dressed in the capes and carrying the ceremonial weaponry acquired on the completion of the initiation ordeal which signified their status as men.*

Ndzundza owed the Boers five years' forced labour. It was little short of slavery. In point of bureaucratic fact, the stipulated terms of the indenture were that each family was to be paid £3 per annum, but since expenses incurred by the farmers were deductible against this sum, many Ndzundza received no money at all – just a patch of land on which to barely subsist.

Moreover, with the war still fresh in their minds, the Boers granted more or less absolute powers to the farmers over their indentured labourers. There was virtually no limit to how hard the Ndzundza could be worked, nor any to the punishments that could be meted out at the least sign of defiance or insubordination. Harsh as their treatment of the defeated Ndzundza was, it should be borne in mind that the Boers themselves perceived it as little more than a survival strategy. Just how much they feared Nyabela and his men is made clear in the 18 July 1883 edition of the ZAR official newspaper, the *Volkstem*, which notes:

> The tribe of Mapoch was regarded by other tribes within and without the Republic as the most powerful in the country ... If [Nyabela] had succeeded in withstanding the Boere forces, it would probably have meant the end of the Transvaal Republic. An alliance of all hostile tribes would probably have followed, which would have made habitation of the country by whites difficult, if not impossible.

Though many of the humiliated Ndzundza were duly released from their servitude at the expiry of the five-year period, as many more were prevented from leaving. Farmers simply refused to let their indentured labourers go, and the government did little to induce them to do so. Even today, more than a century later, there are labourers working on farms in areas like Roossenekal, Stoffberg and Witbank, whose conditions have not changed since their ancestors were indentured in 1883. In researching this book, we spoke to members of the Ndzundza who had never received a day's wage for the labour of a lifetime. We spoke to others, who after generations of living and working on a particular farm – and with no recourse whatever to either custom or law – had been told to pack up and be gone by the next day. In nearly all the white farming areas where the Ndzundza still live, informants told us that physical assault by the descendants of the ZAR Boers on the descendants of the followers of Nyabela remained a commonplace of life. The harsh rule of victor over vanquished can take centuries, it appears, to undo. Life was scarcely easier for those of the Ndzundza who were set free

at the end of their five-year indenture. They were left to fend for themselves how and where best they could. Many of these dispossessed continued to wander nomadically for generations. They moved from place to place, finding piecework on farms and grazing for the few cattle they had somehow been able to keep or accumulate. Then they would be forced to move on again. Only in the 1970s with the establishment of the KwaNdebele homeland were such nomads able to put down roots again.

Others found permanency more quickly. In 1888 some Ndzundza gravitated towards the farm Hartebeestfontein outside Pretoria, where the royal heir Fene, together with his mother and a group of key royal advisors had escaped before the fall of KoNomtjharhelo in 1883. It was here too that Nyabela had moved when, in an act of clemency, he was released from prison in 1899, only to die four years later in 1903. By this stage the Ndzundza monarchy had already begun to re-establish its authority, though in desperately reduced circumstances. (The king himself had to toil as a farm labourer.) When, a few years later, Fene was transferred to the farm Welgelegen on the Wilge River, more of the wandering Ndebele – despite the objections of the white farmers – moved there to establish unsanctioned settlements in the area.

It was only in 1923, the year after Fene's death, that the beginnings of a permanent solution were found. Followers of the new king, Mayisha, were able to scrape up enough money to buy the farm Weltevreden in the Denilton district, northeast of Pretoria. In time this settlement was to become one of the most important Ndzundza Ndebele gathering points, and even today the rambling village which stands there still, houses the royal homestead.

Another locality to which the Ndzundza moved was in the vicinity of Kafferskraal, in the area where the Ndzundza had lived before they moved to Roossenekal in the 1840s. Here a half-brother of Nyabela had established himself as leader, calling himself the rightful heir to the paramount chieftaincy. Forced out by white farmers, this group moved north in 1938 to settle in the Nebo district of the northeastern Transvaal. Here their property rights were formally acknowledged in 1956, when the South African government granted them land under the designated Nebo Farms Trust. More recently, and with scant regard for the ethnicity that was the supposed motivation for its homeland policy, the apartheid government of the National Party unceremoniously bundled these trust farms, together with the lands occupied by groups of Sotho-speakers, into the 'ethnic' homeland of Lebowa. Those mentioned above were not the only Ndzundza settlements that grew up scattered around the Transvaal

*OPPOSITE: A married woman in full tribal regalia as recorded by Constance Stuart Larrabee in the 1950s. She is wearing a beaded marriage blanket or* nguba. *The mace she is holding is used in dancing and is believed to serve as a conducting rod for the energies of the ancestors.*

*PAGES 20-21: A front and back view of an Ndebele bride in 1923. The goatskin bridal cape she wears is known as a* linaga *and is not to be confused with the* nguba, *which is made after marriage. On her head the woman wears a bridal veil or* isiyaya, *which is sometimes extended with tassels to cover the face. The beaded bridal veil is known as an* nyoga, *meaning 'snake'. This veil is never worn in front however, as shown on page 20.*

after the release of the indentured labourers, but with the passage of time most of the others have more or less disappeared. It is therefore mainly on the white farmlands between Roossenekal and Middelburg, and in the area around Weltevreden and the Nebo district, that the arts and culture characteristic of the Ndebele have flourished.

Although this is not the place to address the issue of wallpainting in any detail, it is worth noting here that the styles of painting recognized and identified as 'Ndebele' came to the fore during this period when the Ndzundza found themselves, so to speak, in the wilderness. Decorative Ndebele designs were first observed in the 1940s on farms around Hartebeestfontein. Ironically, they developed to fuller articulation when the Hartebeest-fontein Ndzundza were moved by the South African government to KwaMsiza, an instant 'traditional village' and tourist attraction, outside Pretoria in the next decade.

One would have expected that the powerful tribal identity manifested by the Ndzundza in their years of exile would have made them strong candidates for a tribal homeland early in the apartheid years, when the ruling National Party sought to fragment South Africa into a loose constellation of ethnic states (under the domination, of course, of a central white government). In fact, when the Promotion of Self Government Act was passed in 1959, the Ndebele were not immediately affected. Part of the reason for this was that the Ndebele kings, Mayisha Cornelius and his successor David Mabusa Mapoch, were not willing to play ball and be instated subject to the apartheid regime. Another was that the government sought to lump together the Ndebele and various other problematic subgroupings, such as the Pedi, in the Lebowa homeland. However, with nationalist feelings stirring strongly around the royal kraal, and the long-term possibility being held out of a separate Ndebele homeland, in 1968 King David finally relented to being formally invested by the South African government as paramount chief of the Ndebele.

In the first instance the granting of tribal authority status to King David Mapoch was within the context of the Lebowa homeland, but by the early 1970s pressure was mounting from various quarters to create a specifically Ndebele homeland. Significantly, white farmers in the Transvaal – those who in earlier decades had resisted the idea of a bantustan for the Ndebele – had taken up the call. Their reasons, however, were far from altruistic, arising as they did out of their concern with the alarming squatter problem caused by the eviction of large numbers of farm labourers then redundant in the face of mechanization. As a result, the Ndzundza tribal authority was

prised loose from Lebowa, and future KwaNdebele Chief Minister S S Skosana put in place at its head. By 1974, the South African government had bought up 51 000 hectares of farmland for consolidation into the new homeland, and a process of resettlement had begun.

Many of the Ndebele were only too happy to move to land they could call their own. Significant numbers of

OPPOSITE: *An Ndebele woman grinding wild spinach leaves in a manner still frequently used today.*
BELOW AND BOTTOM: *Constance Stuart Larrabee's record of an Ndebele settlement in the 1950s.*

ABOVE: *A view through the gateway of a homestead at KwaMsiza village. Specifically created by the government as a tourist village, this settlement nevertheless represented one of the definitive flowerings of the Ndebele wall-painting tradition. The 'living museum' at KwaMsiza was discontinued when the National Party government redrew the borders to include the Ndebele settlement in the Tswana homeland of Bophuthatswana.*

farmworkers and those who had been evicted from farms moved of their own accord. Many more, though, were forcibly moved by agents of the central government, often at gunpoint, from the urban and peri-urban areas where they had gravitated to find work, and were simply dumped in the new homeland, without facilities and in unfamiliar places, merely to satisfy the National Party's vision of ethnic separatism. As just one example of the magnitude of the resettlement programme and the government's stolid commitment to it: by 1979 10 000 families had forcibly been moved from the squatter settlement at Winterveld, outside Pretoria, to KwaNdebele.

Initially the idea was that the territory would become more or less self-supporting. Factories would be built and favourable terms created for foreign investors to build industries in the designated area around the capital of KwaMahlangu. Such investment, however, failed to materialize, and the residents of the homeland had still to seek employment in the cities.

The result of the government's social engineering was powerfully documented by photographer David Gold-blatt in the 1980s: people spending up to eight hours a day commuting by bus to their places of employment. Many would set out at three and four o'clock in the morning, only reaching home again at nine and ten at night. These daily migrants sometimes lost as much as half of their wages to travel costs.

Whatever the human cost, the legislative assembly of the new homeland was functioning by 1981, and plans were already being fomented, under the guidance of two white Pretoria-appointed advisors, for granting the homeland its 'independence'.

It was not long before tensions began to develop between the Skosana regime on the one hand and the populace, together with the royal house, on the other. Part of the reason for this lay in the way in which Skosana and his cronies approached the business of governing, which was primarily as a means to self-enrichment. By the early 1980s, members of the legislative assembly and their families owned nearly half of the business economy of the territory, and more or less exclusively controlled the public funds made available through the KwaNdebele Development Corporation.

Then the Skosana regime attempted the unthinkable. With King David Mapoch increasingly siding with the people in resisting the excesses of the Skosana government, a plot was hatched by Skosana and his white advisors to undo King David's paramount chieftaincy. The idea was to delve back into the mythology of the Ndebele and find an excuse for declaring the more compliant Manala leader paramount chief of the nation. Though unsuccessful (not only was the king's office inviolable in the eyes of the people, but the late king enjoyed enormous personal prestige among his subjects), the attempt markedly hardened growing resistance to Chief Minister Skosana and his unelected government.

The crisis came with announcements by State President P W Botha regarding KwaNdebele's proposed independence in 1985 and 1986. With powerful waves of black nationalist resistance sweeping through the country in the wake of the student uprisings of 1976, and with democratic ideals spreading like wildfire via such organizations as the United Democratic Front and the Congress of South African Trade Unions, there could scarcely have been a worse time to attempt to impose such a sham independence upon the Ndebele people.

Given the concatenation of circumstances, the only way to achieve such a move was by force – and force was a means Skosana was not averse to using. Already, in the late 1970s, groups of vigilantes had gathered around Skosana and his clique within the ruling Mbokotho party, and by the mid-1980s they had been involved in dozens of brutal acts of repression against the legislative assembly's political opponents. Student leaders and dissident members of the royal household had been specifically targeted for vicious assault by Skosana supporters – who enjoyed a seeming immunity from the law and often were reported to have acted in concert with Skosana's own police and with the South African security forces who continued to maintain a strong presence in the homeland.

Then in August 1985, State President P W Botha announced the planned incorporation into KwaNdebele of the predominantly Pedi-speaking area of Moutse – at the time part of Lebowa – as a preliminary step towards independence. Violence erupted on all sides. Not only did the Ndebele themselves come into conflict with Skosana and his vigilantes, but so too did the residents of Moutse. Matters came to a head on the first day of 1986 when Skosana's vigilantes swooped on the area, burning houses, killing 26 people and abducting – and then severely assaulting at their leisure – another 400.

Although the residents of Moutse were able to take the question of incorporation to the Supreme Court and have it overturned, resistance to Skosana was no less powerful at home. Skosana's response was to further empower his thugs, and in January 1986 the Mbokotho were formally constituted as a para-governmental 'Ndebele cultural' organization – with special legal status and protection. Outright civil war followed. On one side was the Skosana regime and on the other was the people, led by the royal family, and in particular the man who was to take over the chief ministership of the homeland, Prince James Mahlangu. By August 1986, 160 people had lost their lives, 300 had been detained by the authorities and hundreds had simply gone missing. Schools had been raided and students had been savagely assaulted.

But by this time the tide had turned: in retaliation the students had destroyed 70 percent of all businesses in KwaNdebele (owned as they were by the Skosana clique), and the homes of 41 representatives in the KwaNdebele legislative assembly had been put to the torch. Faced with such destruction the legislative assembly had little option but to back down, and especially after the death on 29 July

of Mbokotho strongman Piet Ntuli. Mbokotho was banned and independence plans were cancelled. In 1988 – a Supreme Court judgment having granted the formerly disenfranchised women of KwaNdebele the right to vote – elections were held for the very first time. The result of these was a landslide victory for the anti-independence party of Prince James Mahlangu, who himself went on to enter the National Assembly as ANC representative in the 1994 democratic elections. Even before then, however, the homeland had been reincorporated by decree into the greater South Africa, thus reversing what remained of the history that the National Party government had sought to construct.

BELOW: *The stark outlining on the buildings in this picture by Constance Stuart Larrabee is suggestive of the strong Sotho influence pervading the development of Ndebele culture, at least since the middle of the 19th century.*

## CHAPTER 2
# BELIEF AND PRACTICE

*In common with most other African peoples, the identity of the Ndebele is conditioned by their belief*
*in the existence of a spirit world in parallel with this one. Particularly important among the denizens of this spirit*
*world are the ancestors of the people. It is they, the Ndebele believe, who demand that the continuities of tradition*
*be maintained and that the rites of bonding through initiation be performed.*

ABOVE: *An Ndebele man reconstructing the male dress of a precolonial past for tourists at the KwaNdebele tourist village near Bronkhorstspruit. Around his neck he wears an* iporiyana, *though such items are seldom as elaborately beaded in real life.*

OPPOSITE: *Mjanyelwa Ndimande-Mtsweni, nyanga and advisor to the king of the Ndebele. He is married to wallpainter Francina Ndimande, and is one of the most important personages in the traditional life of the Ndzundza Ndebele. His necklace of power is made from a python's spine and is punctuated with claws and teeth of slain wild beasts.*

T he Ndebele, like many African tribal groupings, live in a world densely – and sometimes terrifyingly – populated with the invisible creatures of the spirit realm. Not only do these include the shades of the dead, but behind the appearances of physical things – animals, plants and even inanimate things such as stones – there is, they believe, a parallel order of spirits which frequently intersects with the world inhabited by humans.

Within such a world view, illness and misfortune – as much as health and good fortune – are perceived not as having natural causalities, but as the result of either interventions from the spirit world or manipulations of that shadow reality, notably by healers and by witches. Thus, even the effects of herbal preparations in healing are understood to be the result of the workings of the spirit of the relevant plant, or root, or whatever. As one healer put it: 'Every thing has a spirit which makes it powerful, and that spirit can be used for good or evil purposes.'

Although the tribal ancestors interact with all people, regardless of their standing, it is only the healers and witches who can *manipulate* the inhabitants of the other world to effect good and harm.

### THE JEALOUS ANCESTORS

Most important of the denizens of the spirit world are the so-called *AmaNdlozi*, the ancestors. They are at once the spirit guardians and the honoured dead of the tribe. In their dealings with humans, the *AmaNdlozi* are, by turns, jealous and solicitous. They demand sacrifice and placation, laying down complex laws to govern the behaviour of the living. Frequently, failure to follow the intricacies of the tribal law and observance as laid down by the ancestors, is believed to be responsible for misfortune. At the same time, the ancestors are overweeningly concerned to protect their descendants and to guarantee the life of the tribe. Thus, so the Ndebele believe, they regularly appear to the living in dreams, giving counsel, providing charms, and warning against impending disaster. By the same token, it is these ancestors who are understood to impart the knowledge of herbs and other medicinal preparations which lie at the core of traditional healing.

Healing will be dealt with in some detail at a later point. Here it is important to note that the cultural life of the Ndebele is inextricably tied up with their belief in the *AmaNdlozi*, and that nearly everything we consider 'traditional' expresses in one way or another the complex of relationships that bind the living with the dead.

What the ancestors demand above all is continuity and the preservation of tribal identity. Every tradition is rooted in the very fact that it is tradition – that this is the way it was done in the past. Within tribal cultures, such justifications are reason enough; traditional usages are precisely what guarantee the continuity of the particular tribal group, and in continuity identity is sustained.

This is oversimplification, of course. Tradition and material culture reflect at the same time the history of the people and its tribal genealogies. There are significant

ABOVE: *Sheboi Mnguni from the village of Wolwekraal in KwaNdebele, wearing the* iporiyana, *which signifies his totemic clan affiliation, along with a more modern token of identification – a miner's helmet. Affixed to the helmet is the image of political leader Prince James Mahlangu, whose 'Will of the Nation Party' was absorbed into the African National Congress after the latter organization was unbanned.*

overlaps in cultural usage among all of the South Nguni tribal groupings, and what is reflected is as much a common heritage as the different nuances peculiar to the various subgroupings. In some areas of culture there is hardly any distinction between different groups at all. Thus, male initiation rites remain closely related among all the South Nguni groupings, with the exception of the Zulu who have not practised circumcision since the early 19th century. Perhaps more telling in establishing commonalities of culture is the fact that Ndebele healers, though working within their own society, will often claim to be guided by a Swazi or Zulu ancestor.

Nevertheless, such observations serve to reinforce rather than question the central point. Both in external observance – like beadwork, adornment and, to a lesser extent, wallpainting – and in secret rites like initiation, cultural usages have the effect of sustaining unity within the tribal group; at the same time they establish commonalities with and differences from the rest of humanity.

## MEN AND BEASTS

The connectedness of Ndebele society to the ancestors informs tribal identity and effects, at the same time, a sorting of the world into categories of 'us' (being the Ndebele) and 'them' (the outside world). The same function, although in narrower ways, can be read out of the practices associated with the totem of the clan.

In the most basic sense, totems are presences in the spirit world – most often of animals (as they are with the Ndebele) but sometimes of fish – which are associated with related groups of humans, be these in the form of clans, sub-clans or broader tribal groupings.

In the case of the Ndebele, it is the clans or, more simply, people with the same surnames, that are associated with the various totemic animal spirits. To mention just a few of the Ndebele clans: people with the surname Mashiane have as their totem the monkey; Mahlangus are associated with the steenbok; Mtswenis with the baboon; and the Sibanyonis with the guinea fowl.

Some informants expressed a belief that this totemic identity translated itself in literal terms and that their characters were somehow connected to those of their animal familiars. Thus a youth with the surname Mashiane explained his success as a stickfighter by saying he possessed, innately, the agility and cunning of a monkey; but for others the connections appeared less literal and more deeply rooted in tribal lore, some of which is expressed in a body of fable nurtured by the elders of the tribe in which animals play the major parts.

Totemic affiliations carry with them a number of practical implications. Among these is a complex of taboos. Tribespeople are prohibited from killing, eating the flesh of, or wearing the skin of their animal totem. Such prohibitions are also carried into the vegetable kingdom, with related taboos being associated with the cutting down or burning of particular trees.

At the same time, rules of marriage and social intercourse are prescribed by totemic affiliation. It is not permitted to marry inside one's own (that is, one's father's) clan. Nor is it permitted to marry inside the local branches of the extended family into which one's mother was born, though remoter relatives are not prohibited.

Even beyond this, there are complexities around totem and surname. Certain clans (for example the Mahlangus) are forbidden to intermarry with other clans (for example the Kabinis), certain jobs are denied the members of particular clans, certain complex rules of interaction are prescribed between particular clans, and so on.

However arcane the associated beliefs and lore may be, the basic principles are simple enough. The animal totem – since it is the father's clan that determines it – is associated with the patriarchies, and it enforces patrilineage and the inheritance of sons. It also, and perhaps more basically, serves to prevent incest and the intermarriage of people closely related to each other genetically. On a more mystical level, it creates a set of linkages and echoes between human society and the world at large, and in this way serves to impose order on the chaos of experience and to integrate the human into the totalities of life.

Despite the importance of totems in the social life and in the personal and group identity of the Ndebele, the part they play in the material culture of the people is severely limited. As far as I am aware at any rate, it is only in items of adornment that are associated with male initiation – notably the *iporiyana*, a breastplate made of animal hide – that totem plays any determinate role in art-making. In the *iporiyana*, the choice of animal skin is only indirectly related to the totem of the wearer. He is, of course, prohibited from wearing the hide of his own totem animal; but at the same time he is *required* to wear the skin of another particular animal (or animals). This is prescribed by tribal lore, the choice of animal (or rather its skin) reflecting the mysteries on which the practice of totemism is based. Mtswenis, for instance, will wear the skin of a hyena on their *iporiyanas* and Ndimandes that of a wild cat. Exactly why a particular animal is chosen is usually obscure – even to the wearer himself: few among the Ndebele today remember the secret totemic narratives of the tribe on which such lores are based.

Be all this as it may, the *iporiyana*, while sometimes embellished with strips of beading, is generally an un-remarkable item. It is something that is made by men in the world of men. And traditionally, it is the Ndebele women who are the artists.

Despite its marginality in relation to the art of the Ndebele, there is good reason for discussing the issue of totem here. Even among professional researchers and academics, it is not generally realized that the Ndebele are totemic in their social organization, and some researchers expressed surprise when I told them what Ndebele men had told me. The reason for this is that the Nguni in general do not have clan totems; such observances are thought to be characteristic of the Sotho-Tswana groups.

Going back to the early migrations which led to the emergence of the Ndebele as a separate grouping, it is evident that the totem was not a tradition carried with them from the common South Nguni stock. This means that the tradition was acquired somewhere along the way through the mixing up of Nguni with some other (almost certainly Sotho-Tswana) gene pool and culture. Like many other features of Ndebele culture – some of the traditions of healing employed by their sangomas, for instance, and most probably wallpainting too – the use of totemic practice strongly suggests that Ndebele culture is far more hybrid and eclectic than is generally thought. It underlines at the same time a crucial but little acknowledged fact: that tradition does not look backwards to the supposed beginning of time, but in fact constantly adapts, transforms and mutates in its passage through time.

## NDEBELE HEALERS

The basis of traditional African healing differs radically from that of Western medicine. While the effects of Western healing are understood to be scientific and chemical in nature, healing in the traditional African context has everything to do with the unseen world of the spirits – just as sickness is thought to be the result of manipulations of the forces residing in the spirit realm.

Among the Ndebele, there are two main types of healer. First, there is the *nyanga*, who is exclusively a herbalist and studies through an apprenticeship the properties of herbal preparations. While the underlying theory guiding the practice of the *nyanga* is derived from the ancestor and spirit realm, he (*nyangas* are always men) acquires his knowledge from study and from the cumulative knowledge of his profession in much the same way as would Western healers. Nevertheless, the parallels should not be taken too far and we should not attempt – as do many

researchers reacting against the Western perception of traditional healers as mere purveyors of mumbo jumbo – to see *nyangas* as working in the same kind of context as Western doctors. While there is a good deal of what our culture would acknowledge as valid medicinal knowledge embedded in the learning of the *nyanga*, there is also a good deal of outright magic. For the *nyanga*, the term 'herbs' embraces also animal and sometimes even human extracts, and when *nyangas* describe the effects of these, the basis is nothing more nor less than sympathetic magic: the dried and ground flesh of lions will ensure strength, snake extracts will instil fear, and so on. Such thinking remains alien to Western empiricism, and it is doubtful that the gulf between the two will ever really be narrowed.

The second type of healer is the sangoma – or, as the West has xenophobically designated that personage, the witchdoctor. This type of traditional healer, while he or she also uses herbs in healing, is above all a specialist in ecstatic possession and, by means of the throwing and interpreting of the 'bones', a diviner. The knowledge that the sangoma possesses is gleaned through communication in dreams and trance states with the ancestors; more particularly, though not exclusively, with a single ancestor who serves as that sangoma's spirit guide. Though most rural Ndebele claim that the ancestors communicate with them on a relatively regular basis in dreams – ordering particular observances, communicating wisdom, or censuring lapses in custom – it is only the sangomas who are able to make contact with the ancestor realm more or less at will.

The path to becoming a sangoma is characterized by a set of circumstances that are observed with remarkable constancy by tribal cultures throughout the world – from the Innuit of the North Pole to the Australian aborigines. Broadly, what this so-called shamanistic healing complex entails is twofold: on the one hand, a vocation that is rooted in illness and thus in privileged access to the world of the dead, and the systematic practise of techniques of ecstatic possession, on the other.

The first step to sangomahood is marked by illness. Often the illness has physical symptoms, like uncontrollable shaking, but at the same time it has elements of what we would call madness. Descriptions of this state vary: some informants talk about being overrun with spiders; others speak of their heads being 'opened up' or cleft with violent pains, others again talk of tormenting dreams or a constant babble of voices. Whatever the symptoms, the result is the same – the ancestor who has thus chosen the sangoma and who will serve as his or her guide in the future, appears to the sufferer and announces the only way

*BELOW AND PAGE 30: The necklaces of power worn by sangomas are partly magical and partly decorative. The necklaces of Elijah Mabena, pictured here, from the Middelburg district, are threaded with beaded* isifiso *or medicine bottles containing herbal preparations; the strings of plastic beads are chosen, he says, on purely aesthetic grounds. The scars on his back are from stick fighting on behalf of his younger brother during the latter's* wela, *or initiation ordeal.*

*PAGE 31: The paraphernalia of the sangoma. Beads, drums, necklaces and herbal preparations belonging to Sophie Ntuli from Waterval village, KwaNdebele.*

ABOVE: *Sophie Ntuli dressed for work as a sangoma. Around her ankles she is wearing strings of a particular insect's larvae, which produce percussive effects in the dance. Her necklace features a number of metal bangles which she wears at the behest of her guardian ancestor. Another sangoma we spoke to was told by the ancestors that she had to wear both metal and wood in combination, or else her powers would desert her.*

to a cure: by taking on the mantle of the sangoma. At this moment, by all accounts, the suffering ceases. But the path to fully fledged sangomahood is far from travelled. The novice is sent to study under an established sangoma who, over a period ranging from one to sometimes three and four years, passes on the secrets of the herbs, and initiates the student into the arcane knowledge of the 'bones'. In the throwing of these — at least three times a day in most cases — the sangoma believes he or she is able to divine the future as well as diagnose sicknesses and prescribe their cure.

Exactly when this period of preparation ends is once again dictated by the ancestors, or so the Ndebele believe. The ancestor guide will appear in a dream either to the student or the elder sangoma and order that the rites of induction now begin.

Throughout the sangoma's career, this ancestor remains his or her link with the truths of the other side. The sangoma Petrus Shabalala from Kwaggafontein, for instance, recounted a series of dreams in which his 'great grandfather' appeared to him. In life, this ancestor had been a sangoma of note and therefore was the owner of a powerful 'bag of medicines' which, many generations down the line, Shabalala had been chosen to inherit. This bag, which he refers to as an almost physical thing, constitutes the basis of his knowledge of the herbs, and, so he believes, guarantees his power as a witchdoctor.

So too, one Elijah Mabena, a sangoma from the Middelburg area, said that in his practice as a sangoma he had adopted the name of a long-dead sangoma called Mahlanbazimuke. As he understood it, with the name went the knowledge and the power of the long-buried healer to the extent that, as a sangoma, he claimed he actually was Mahlanbazimuke.

These mysterious connections are both cemented and celebrated in an all-night initiation ritual. Along with other sangomas, the initiate will imbibe a special and powerfully hallucinogenic foam of vegetable origin. Then, accompanied by drums, which are an essential part of the apparatus of the sangoma, the group will enter into a protracted phase of ecstatic dancing. In the dance, they believe the ancestors enter their bodies and possess them.

Finally, there comes the time for the ceremony of initiation itself. This is centred around the sacrifice of a female goat — whose colour and physical appearance will have been prescribed beforehand by the guiding ancestor. In a peculiarly African kind of Communion ceremony, the initiate drinks first from the warm blood of the slaughtered beast — whose mouth and anus have been stuffed to magical effect with herbs — then eats of its flesh. At this point

the full powers and status of the sangoma are ritually invested and the initiate may now practise his or her skills among the people at large. A knuckle bone from the sacrificial goat is kept as a token of the ceremony of investiture and as the focal point of the sangoma's powers.

## BEADS AND SYMBOLS OF POWER

Various external symbols are employed to sustain the powers of the sangoma within the tribe. Some are worn only in ritual and ceremonial circumstances, some at all times. First among these is a simple string of beads — in most cases alternating red with white, but sometimes interspersed with black, green, blue and other colours.

Sophie Ntuli, one of the most important of the sangomas in the KwaNdebele territory, identified the colours of her beading by referring to different sangoma traditions. The white, she explained, invoked the Nguni traditions of medicine, the red the Ndau traditions, and the blue the wisdom of the kings. Each, she continued, was associated with a different set of remedies and a distinct body of guiding ancestor spirits.

To elaborate: the Nguni tradition is that of herbal medicine, healing by means of preparations extracted from plants and from the dried flesh of animals. Those healers who practise only this tradition are referred to as *nyangas,* but when the witchdoctor practises also the shamanistic mysteries of 'the drum', then he or she is referred to as a sangoma. The Ndau tradition is one of divination and is probably not of Nguni origin; it takes its name from a tribal grouping who today live in central Mozambique and Zimbabwe. Directed towards what we might call 'fortune telling' and the seeking out of the causes of maladies and also their remedies — all of which, for its practitioners, are inextricably tied up with communication with the ancestors — the Ndau tradition is connected with the practices of ecstatic dancing too, and thus with the sangoma's mystical drum. The word sangoma in fact translates as 'person of the drum', and on initiation the sangoma receives a drum specially treated with magical herbs and ritual invocations. This serves simultaneously as a symbol of sangoma status and as a channel to the spirit realm.

In every case, the drum is used as a musical accompaniment to the dancing which induces those trance states in which the spirits are able to channel their messages through the shaman. In many cases, such as the practices of sangomas of the Ndau tradition, the music of the drum is accompanied by the imbibing of hallucinogenic substances. The other aspect of the Ndau tradition is that of divination by means of the witchdoctor's bones. These bones, as will be discussed in more depth later, are generally put together from sacrifices performed by the sangoma (one from each act of healing through sacrifice), and they function essentially as symbols through which the ancestors are able to communicate with the living. Though most sangomas possessing the gift of the Ndau will claim that the ancestors communicate in dreams and trances, and sometimes in everyday life, it is in the arrangements of the bones as thrown by the sangoma that the ancestors are believed to communicate their messages to the community at large.

Finally, in the list provided by Sophie Ntuli, there is 'the wisdom of the kings'. This is a highly secret body of knowledge and, as far as can be ascertained, is made up of a jealously guarded collection of stories and founding myths. On a number of occasions, we encountered women who referred to such a collection of stories as having been secreted by the royal entourage and therefore unavailable to the common person. These, we were told, explained and justified the laws and observances of the Ndebele, but nowhere were we able to discover their content. But to the wearer of the blue beads, such knowledge, and the healing lore that goes with it, is readily available, channelled from a royal ancestor guide.

The white, red and blue beads referred to above were not the only bead colours that we saw associated with sangomas, but in many cases the significance of the beads appeared purely personal – a usage either prescribed by the particular guiding ancestor, or just deployed to decorative effect. It is possible anyway to make too much of their meaning. The institution of the sangoma, like most institutions in Ndebele culture, is susceptible to individual nuances. And to confuse matters further, the symbolism associated with the beads is not constant. The symbolism of the red and the white beads can even be reversed, with the white being used in some contexts to invoke the Ndau traditions of herbalism.

In short, there is no universal, overriding pattern to the appurtenances of the sangoma, but this should not be thought of as detracting in any way from the seriousness of sangomahood or its outward displays. Many of the sangomas spoken to said misfortune would certainly befall them should they fail to wear their beads and sacrificial goat knuckle bone at all times; some went as far as to express the belief that they would die.

In addition to the beads, there are a number of other pieces of regalia distinctive to the sangoma. One is the dancing wand, which, in terms of the belief system, functions as a kind of lightning conductor to the ancestor realm. Without this, sangomas are unable to dance or to approach the trance states in which communication with the revered dead becomes possible.

Perhaps the most interesting of the items worn by the sangoma, from an artistic point of view, is the necklace of power. This combines a variety of esoteric items strung together and interspersed with various types of beads. Notably, it includes a series of beaded horns and tiny calabashes which contain herbal preparations and various animal essences, most often from snakes, elephants, rhinoceroses and crocodiles. Such magically charged containers are referred to as *izifiso*, or 'wishes'.

The variety of items displayed in sangoma necklaces is wide, to say the least, but the basic intent is constant: to at once signal the powers of the wearer and, in magical ways, to protect and empower him or her. To wear is to possess, and to possess is to control the spirit of the thing you wear. Thus, for example, many sangomas wear snake essences in their *izifiso*, in the belief that they will take on some of the characteristics of snakes. Operatively, they expect to be universally feared, just as snakes are universally feared. At the same time they believe they will be immune from harm emanating from these reptiles. In a peculiarly atavistic sense, you are what you wear.

In addition to all this, necklaces of power will often include pieces of wood (the types of which will have been specified by the ancestors on an individual basis) interspersed with metal elements such as safety pins and nails. The reason for this is related to a wider symbolism proper to the sangoma, and indeed to shamanistic peoples the world over: within the traditional world view, wood is related to female energies, while metal is distinctively male. By wearing both wooden and metal elements the sangoma is acting out the capacity to heal both males and females and to harness both energies within the medicine.

But while all these symbolic potencies are being enacted in the necklace of power, so, often, is something more secular and appealing. For many of the sangomas, particularly the younger ones, the necklace of power becomes a site for decorative artistic play. Plastic beads are frequently introduced in bright profusions, as are Victorian-style lucky charms, together with various other extraneous bits and pieces; the overall effect of the necklace as an aesthetic object is therefore often as festive as it is hieratic, as funky 'third-world' as it is 'traditionally African'.

### SOPHIE NTULI'S BONES

Of all the practices of sangomahood, perhaps the hardest for the Western mind to accept is that of the stock-in-trade of Hollywood's Africa, the witchdoctor's bones.

BELOW: *Sophie Ntuli throws the bones. The stick protruding into the picture from the left belongs to her assistant, Petrus Shabalala, who assists her in the reading of the omens.*

BELOW: *Ndimande-Mtsweni in everyday dress at his cattle byre. The stick he holds is the one he uses for hunting pythons. Such magically charged implements are not allowed within the confines of the homestead.*

BOTTOM RIGHT: *Ndimande-Mtsweni in traditional male attire. His headpiece, he said, is not specifically associated with his high office, but merely an ancient traditional usage. The only signal of his pre-eminence is given by the python-spine necklace of power.*

OPPOSITE: *Piet Mashiane from Weltevrede dressed in the outfit his father made on Piet's return from the wela: his attainment of full manhood. Around his neck is the iporiyana of his clan, on his shoulders a goatskin cape and on his head a cap similarly made of goatskin which, though slouched in this instance, is more usually pointed. The spear is a symbolic and optional extra.*

Nevertheless, whatever reason might have to say on the subject, Sophie Ntuli and her apprentice, Petrus Shabalala, did know beforehand that we were coming. The bones, when they threw them earlier that day, 'told them', they said. Then, throwing the bones again Sophie Ntuli pointed to three wire-wound goat's knuckle bones. These, they said, identified their three male visitors. Then Sophie Ntuli pointed with her foot-shaped stick to a commercially polished seashell in a clear conjunction with these goat knuckles. This shell, Sophie explained, because of its connection with the oceans, intimates the arrival of whites or foreigners.

The lesson went on to include all sorts of prognostications of good fortune and great wealth – which, unfortunately for us, have not yet materialized. But such observations by the sangomas should perhaps be taken more as tokens of good manners and good humour, alas, than as literal predictions.

Nonetheless, the demonstration, performed as it was in an utterly matter of fact and demystified manner, with doves cooing fit to burst in the background and passers-by calling out greetings from the street, was enough to give pause – and to prompt some close attention as Sophie and her apprentice explained.

A sangoma's bag of bones serves simultaneously as the healer's basic divinatory tool and as a kind of portfolio of witchdoctoring. Each sacrifice that has been performed under the sangoma's auspices is recorded by the addition to his or her collection of a single bone. In most cases – though some are left plain, merely sun-bleached – the bone is treated in one of two ways: either it is beaded or it is wound with wire. If beaded, it signifies a woman or a female energy. If wound with wire – metals powerfully invoking the male within the shamanistic consciousness – it refers to a man. These, then, are used as the basic pointers, and according to their conjunction with other items will suggest different divinatory meanings.

Together with these 'identifiers' is a collection of what one might call 'signifiers' – objects that suggest interpretations to be worked up around those pointed out by the bones. Some of these are expectably 'African'. In her bag of bones Sophie Ntuli includes, for example, a number of beaded cow horns which have been treated with herbs and kept as charms against the various maladies that afflicted the animals from which the horns were taken. In some cases these maladies are disease-related, but in others the issue is more metaphysical, and one horn that she identified had been hacked from a cow struck by lightning and now serves as a prophylactic against that fate.

Alongside such items there is another class of objects which, at first glance, fit uncomfortably in the traditional healer's instrument bag. There is a piece of Lego, a domino, a die, a cowrie shell, an old one-cent piece, seemingly random pieces of plastic, and so on. As Sophie Ntuli discusses them, though, the incongruity dissolves. The domino speaks of money. The curio conch shell stands for foreigners, the Lego for building... .

The significance to be extracted from this is that Sophie Ntuli's sangoma practice is not something static. Her bones needs must incorporate and adapt in such a way that they can deal with the exigencies of the largely non-traditional world in which, historically, she lives. In a world of plastic and motor cars and guns she needs to be able to divine around plastic and motor cars and guns. Only such adaptation and inclusiveness will ensure – for the sangoma, as for the other institutions of Ndebele culture – the survival of the tradition.

## A SUPERSANGOMA

Mjanyelwa Ndimande-Mtsweni does not use a drum and he does not dance. Neither was he chosen as a sangoma via the usual route of illness and madness. He did not need to go through such routines, he says. 'I did not become sick because I already knew something about

these things.' As a boy he had already been chosen, assisting his sangoma grandfather from a young age, learning about the herbs and their uses; then he simply went on from there. Nevertheless, Ndimande-Mtsweni does throw the bones, even though he refers to himself only as an *nyanga* or herbalist.

Yet Ndimande-Mtsweni, husband of the mural artist Francina Ndimande, is the most powerful sangoma of all among the Ndebele. He is chief advisor to Cornelius, reigning king of the Ndebele, and he was advisor to Cornelius's father, King David Mapoch, and to David's father before that. It is he who oversees the rites of passage involved in the Weltevrede male initiation, and it is he who actually performs the ritual circumcision which is their focal point.

Mjanyelwa Ndimande-Mtsweni is a remarkable-looking man, with his traditional top tuft of hair, the single red bead threaded through a specially grown lock of hair and hanging in the middle of his forehead – and the bizarre, atavistic necklace of power suspended around his neck. It is made from the vertebral column of a python, and on this weirdly beautiful string there are attached the tooth of a crocodile, the claw of a lion, and a horn containing rhinoceros and crocodile fats and ground elephant bone, all mixed up with herbs.

All of these creatures, he says, he has killed himself, using herbal preparations to 'tame' them, then strangling them with wire hoops, or clubbing them with prepared sticks. Such hunting excursions, he explains, formed an essential part of his preparation. In slaying the beasts and reptiles in question, he has taken on their various powers; he has, in his words, 'tamed' them on a cosmological level, and is now not only himself immune from their threat but also magically able to bend them to his will.

There is more to his relationship with the world of animal spirits than that, though. When he describes the hunting of the crocodile, Ndimande-Mtsweni spins a tale that sounds at first like deranged nonsense. He tells of moving into the waters, becoming a kind of water-being, living for months without air. He talks of dying, then, alive once again, creating a snare, treating it with herbs and finally strangling the crocodile with a loop of cord.

What Ndimande-Mtsweni is describing is the highest mystery of the traditional healer, an inexplicable death and rebirth in water, which, whether one wants to take it literally or metaphorically, gives the practitioner sustained access to the 'other side'. Returning from the world of the dead, the sangoma is accorded the title of *isanusi* as he or she is believed to have acquired the status and the powers of a denizen of that higher world of the spirits. He or she

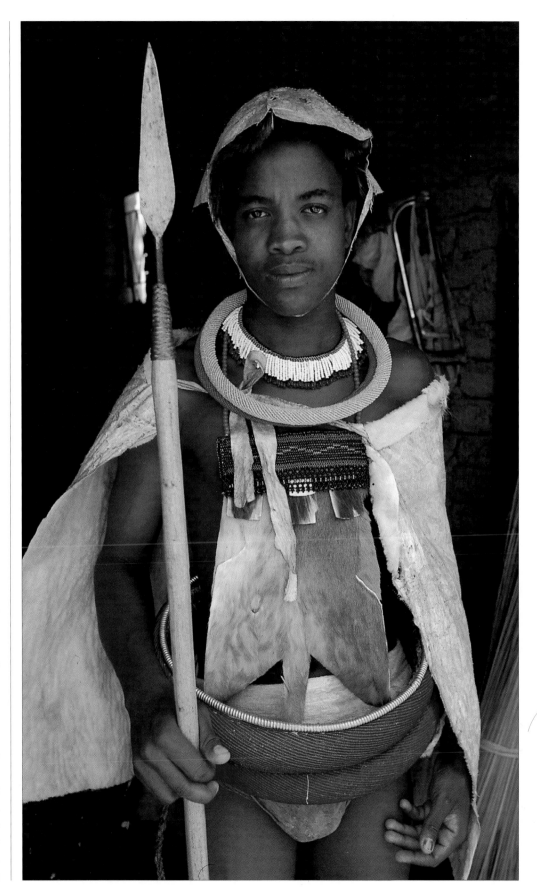

is believed to have made a quantum leap to become something like an ancestor on the earth, and with this goes a transcendence of the laws and particularities of this life.

Our formal interview concluded, Ndimande-Mtsweni takes us outside the walls of the homestead and unfurls a python skin four to five metres long. He points into a tree, where the still moist flesh of the reptile is hanging up to dry so that it can be turned into medicines. Then we are taken to the cattle kraal – protected, he notes, with python fat – where he keeps his collection of herbally treated hunting sticks, such implements not being allowed within the walls of the homestead. The one that he uses against pythons is barely more substantial than a broomstick.

## INITIATION

Initiation for both males and females marks the passage from child to adult status within the tribal context. At the conclusion of the rites, the initiate is permitted to become sexually active and to enter into the usually protracted process of engagement and marriage.

The rites of passage also serve to bond the age groups of the tribe together and separate them from members of other age groups. Thus, one of the powerful injunctions that is given in the male initiation process is that the initiate should henceforth mix only with men who have undergone the initiation trial, and on no account should he reveal to pre-initiates the secrets of what actually happens during the period of seclusion in the bush. At the same time the initiate is taught that every father is his father, every mother within the tribal unit his mother. What this entails – and parallel prohibitions and teachings apply in the case of the female initiation – is a powerful stratification of society into levels of life-attainment. Thus is a vertical structuring of society effected.

Initiation serves also as an induction into the mysteries and the lore of the tribe. In both male and female initiation rituals, an important part is played by post-initiates whose task it is to impress upon the neophytes the nature and importance of tribal lore. Then, with the next cycle of initiations, the newly initiated are the ones chosen to play the role of guides, and thus the transfer of knowledge is carried down through time.

### MALE INITIATION

The rites of male initiation – or, to give it its Ndebele names, *wela* or *ingoma* – are performed among the Ndzundza Ndebele only once every four years. The long process begins as it ends – at the kraal of the Ndzundza king, when the fathers of boys of an appropriate age approach the king and nominate their sons for the forth-coming *ingoma*. The boys are usually between 15 and 18 years of age but there is no absolute limit, and occasionally young men in their twenties have yet to undergo the rite. The reason for this is often that there are a number of sons closely spaced within the family and only one son is allowed to be initiated each time.

Once the participants have been registered, the king sets a specific date, and for three weeks before that date the neophytes – usually ignorant of what lies in store – don headbands of plaited grass known as *izisonyana* in token of their preparation. While thus attired the neophyte has a number of ritualized tasks to perform. He is required to pay a visit to his grandparents to inform them that he is about to go to the bush and become a man. He is also required to visit the graves of his forefathers in order to make libations. He takes with him a calabash of traditional beer, drinks half, then pours the other half on the graves, before speaking to the ancestors and asking their protection in the coming months. Finally, on the day before the ordeal actually begins, the would-be initiate approaches his mother, formally informing her of his intentions, and she answers with an equally formal reply, telling her son to go but to come back again, and assuring him that she will beg the ancestors to keep him safe.

Just before the boys actually depart, still wearing the *izisonyana*, they don a loincloth made of animal skin. Clad only in this and with a single blanket, though it is winter when the initiation rites begin, they proceed to the king's kraal. Here the younger boys in the tribe come, in ritualized procession, to look on their brothers for the last time before they become men.

Once the younger boys have left, the initiates are despatched to a house designated as that of an important female tribal ancestor, to spend their last night in communion with the spirits that will guide them in the months to come. At around 1 am the next morning, they are summoned, and wrapped in blankets, and with eyes downcast – so as to cut them off from their usual village life – they move in single file back to the king's kraal.

Then they are taken to a sacred place at the river, accompanied by their fathers and other men from the tribe, all armed with guns, pangas and other weapons. The reason for the weapons soon becomes clear: it is so that none of the boys can run away when they discover what is about to happen.

This is circumcision, performed one by one on the boys by a man specially appointed by the king. Though it can be any man, in recent years it has been performed by Mjanyelwa Ndimande-Mtsweni, the king's *nyanga*.

Led by their fathers to a particular, sacred rock, the boys are brutally cut without either warning or anaesthetic.

'He does it with an okapi (a trademarked clasp knife), an old one, not even sharp,' one informant said. 'If he doesn't do it right you can die, but the fathers just say don't cry. You want to be a man so don't cry. This is our tradition, we have all come from there.'

By all accounts wishing they had died, the boys, still under escort, embark on what must be a peculiarly excruciating march of some 10 miles into the bush where they will remain for the next three months. They are divided into groups according to their villages of origin and deposited in various localities in the bush. Here each of the novitiates is met by an elder brother – usually a brother who endured the rites of passage the last time they took place, four years earlier – or, in the absence of a blood relative, a young man from the village specially designated for the task.

These brothers will play an important role in the months that follow. By the time the initiates – *abakwetha*, or chosen ones, as they are known in the vernacular – arrive in the bush, a shelter, known as an *mphandu*, has already been constructed for them by these elder guides. In the following weeks, once the men have returned to

OPPOSITE: *Piet Mashiane's elder brother Jerry, aged 28, in the ceremonial attire of manhood. It was Jerry who ministered to Piet and fought with sticks for the honour of his younger brother in the ritualized violence of the* wela. *With him is his youngest brother, who one day will also undergo the ordeal – if tradition holds that long.*

ABOVE: *The Mashiane brothers, Jerry and Piet, go through the motions of the stick fighting that elder brothers engage in during the* wela, *or three-month initiation process.*

washed and given an application of salt, which despite the increased pain does serve as some kind of antiseptic. For the first two weeks, informants told us, they are not allowed to eat solids, nor even (for the first week) to drink water, subsisting solely on cooked pumpkin flesh.

'We ask why our brothers will not give us water to drink, but they say if you drink water or if you smoke while you are still bleeding, you will see things that are not there. You will go mad.'

These first weeks are, above all, a mystical endurance test. If you die, or if your penis gets infected, it is because, as the Ndebele chillingly explain it, your blood was 'bad'. Such bad blood can result from floutings of taboo dating generations back, or it can be the consequence of personal sins against tradition. Primary among these, so the Ndebele believe, is having indulged in sexual activity prior to the sanctions given by the rituals of manhood.

Thus does the tribe explain the mortality rate among initiates which we would ascribe to the shockingly un-hygenic conditions of the circumcision. Thus also, by inculcating a sense of guilt and blame among the suffering youth, do they ensure that the vast majority of them would rather die in the bush than seek medical attention. In this way a shroud of shame and secrecy is wrapped around the deaths – which undoubtedly occur each time a group of youths endures the rites of passage – and this prevents any statistics from becoming available. However, each time the Nguni initiations take place – the basic procedure is similar among the Swazi and Xhosa – reports appear in the African press of deaths and mutilations. In recent years these have come increasingly to the fore as youths defy the pressures of tradition and peer group, and seek medical attention at Western hospitals for the infections that set in. In the last decade or so, more and more youths have been circumventing the tradition, instead booking into hospitals for the circumcision that will identify them as men.

In the third week, if the *abakwetha* has survived thus far, his diet is expanded to include some meat. In the first instance this is provided by the fathers of the initiates, who club together to buy animals, which are then slaughtered by their elder sons. When this supply runs out, the youths are left to their own devices, eating only what they can hunt or glean from the land.

Throughout this period, the elder brothers pass on the laws of the tribe and the ancestors, the mythologies of initiation, the founding myths of the society and so on, as the group congregates around campfires at night. Mainly, it is a sense of membership of the tribal group and its stratifications that is passed down. To reinforce the sense

ABOVE: *A group of boys during their initiation as recorded by Constance Stuart Larrabee in the 1950s.*

their villages and while the *abakwetha* recover from their wounds, they are nursed by their brothers and each night taken down to the river to enact a cleansing ceremony which serves simultaneously ritual and practical functions. The initiates, wearing nothing but their loincloths, go down in procession to the river at three and four in the morning, singing praise songs to their forefathers. When they get there they ritually cleanse themselves in the icy waters, still offering up praises, before their penises are of belonging, a secret language is adopted – basically gibberish – in which words are spoken backwards. Even after returning from the bush this language is used by groups of men to exclude non-initiates from their conversation.

'The law,' as one recent initiate put it, 'is one law. When you go back you are a man, and when you are a man, you must not mix with a boy who has not been through this thing. You must also know that every father in the village is your father and every mother is your mother, and you must respect what they say.'

Thus the initiation rites continue for the first two months, broken only by visits paid by initiated male relatives. At equally irregular intervals the *nyanga* who is overseeing the *wela* will also arrive to instruct the youths.

In the third month the pattern changes dramatically. The initiates embark upon a highly ritualized game of hide and seek with their mothers, who at this point make the (equally ritualized) journey to seek out their sons.

Explaining the rules according to which the ensuing theatre proceeds, one of our sources said: 'Our mothers have not seen us for a long time, so they are going to come and look for us. At this time we wear goatskin caps on our heads and black skin for our underpants. We smear white stuff like lime on our heads and our bodies, so our mothers when they see us will not be able to say, "That one, that one is my son." [Once] they have seen us we disappear into the bush ... [but] come back to play hide and seek with them again.

'Then there comes a time when our brothers say, "Now you are going to play and we go out into the bush, where our mothers have come to look for us". Our mothers know that we are eight in the group, so they come to see if there are still eight, to make sure one has not died. So when we come out of the bush, a long way away from them, they can count how many we are. If it is eight it is all right, but if there are only seven they can't see which one is missing.'

No doubt there is this practical aspect to the procedure. But at the same time, one might speculate, what is being acted out here is a powerfully rooted ambivalence among the men of the Ndebele in relation to their women. On the one hand there is much said about respect for the mothers and the grandmothers and the female ancestors, but on the other there is a powerful belief in the role of witches. As one informant explained: 'If you see a woman out there in the bush, you must know she is a witch,' and he proceeded to recount a story deeply embedded in the lore surrounding initiation.

'There was one group, they were 11 and they were of one party. The day comes when it is raining, and the lightning strikes. They see a woman in the light, but when the lightning strikes again, there is no woman there. Then number one to number 10 of that party all die and only one of them, who was given powerful medicine before going to the bush, is still alive at the end. The medicine has made him strong and so the witches cannot harm him, but the others die because the witches have poured poison in that place and it is too strong for them.'

At more or less the same time as the initiates embark on their game of hide and seek with the mothers, the elder brothers enter into a period in which they engage in ritualized battles, two by two against one another. In these gladiatorial contests, which continue through the entire last month, the brothers are armed with long sticks made into whips by the attachment of a thinner, suppler stick at the end, and with shields made of animal hide.

Though ritualized, these stickfights are real enough – as the crisscross lines of battle scars worn on their backs and torsos by young men who have served as initiation brothers bear witness. They are fought, so informants told us, on behalf of the antagonists' younger brothers, and it is the honour of these, the initiates, that is at stake. If the brother fights well, by a process of transfer the glory reflects on the initiate, and he will be brave and strong too. The honour of the bloodline – and this in the end is of greater significance to the Ndebele than the individual – will have been upheld. At the next round of initiations, the novitiate will have the opportunity to prove his own valour when he fights for his younger brother's honour.

By this time the *ingoma* is all but over. The king calls all the fathers together and announces the date on which the initiation is going to end.

While the *wela* has been in progress, life has not been going on at home in the usual way. This is the time that, in the traditional framework, houses are painted in anticipation of the newly-made man's return. Often an addition is built on to the homestead for the son, now needing his own room, to move into on his return.

At the same time the mother will be working to produce the *linga koba* which she will wear in bittersweet celebration of her son's ascent to manhood. This piece of regalia comprises a pair of long, narrow bead strips, which hang on either side of the head and are connected by a thong which fits over the crown of the wearer. Beautifully named the 'long tears', the *lingakoba* is worn by women whose sons have become men, and is understood as embodying the mother's simultaneous pride at having borne a man and sadness at having lost a boy. In addition to the above preparations, there is the considerable business of collecting and paying for the presents that will be

BELOW: *At the eye of the storm: King Cornelius of the Ndzundza, who every fourth year orders the* wela, *was formerly Minister of Health in the KwaNdebele homeland government. Despite a growing medical outcry, he believes that circumcision by the traditional method should be retained.*

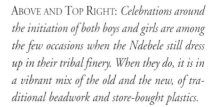

ABOVE AND TOP RIGHT: *Celebrations around the initiation of both boys and girls are among the few occasions when the Ndebele still dress up in their tribal finery. When they do, it is in a vibrant mix of the old and the new, of traditional beadwork and store-bought plastics.*

sunset on the appointed day the young men return to the chief's kraal, tightly wrapped in new blankets, eyes downcast, in single file, exactly as they left three months earlier – except that they are now wearing, hanging down between their buttocks, a strip of animal hide known as a *stiritimba*, a triumphant symbol of manhood, made by their grandfathers.

Forbidden to enter the kraal of the king, the initiates wait at the gate, until that personage appears to give his blessing and put the formal stamp on their attainment of full manhood. At this point the young men are no longer bound by their initiation and a feast in their honour is held that night by the king. Then, as a final ceremony, the youths go down to the river for the last time at sunrise the next day, for one further ceremonial cleansing. Then the group disperses, the boys from each respective village returning home.

In each village there is a long round of celebrations to attend – one hosted by the family of each of the intitiates, at which the entire group of initiates sleep over each time, and a few assorted others. Only at the end of this cycle of parties do the young men return home. When they do, animals are slaughtered and sacrificed by the parents to the ancestors for the protection afforded their son. Once this has been done the initiate takes the stomach of a cow to the home of his grandmother and formally announces that what he promised has now come to pass, that he is now a man, no longer a boy. Finally, he returns to the graves of his ancestors to offer a libation of traditional beer and to give thanks for the protection he has received over the past months.

Now he is recognized as a fully fledged adult and he is free to become engaged to be married, he is free to engage in (limited) sexual intercourse. In many cases, however, he is unable. We spoke to youths who had undergone the rites of initiation more than half a year earlier and whose penises had yet to properly heal. Others, we were told, had been permanently deformed. Nevertheless, the traditions of the tribe had once again been upheld.

### FEMALE INITIATION

After the horrific ordeal that is male initiation, the rites by which girls pass into adulthood are relatively gentle and nurturing. There is no clitorodectomy performed, nor any bodily mutilation. The girls are kept at home – albeit in a specially constructed room and in isolation from the rest of the world – and the worst they have to endure is long periods of solitude and ritual cleansings down by the river. Where male initiation is a group experience, each girl goes through her seclusion alone, though there may be many

given to the young man in celebration of his ordeal. Such gifts will vary considerably depending on the wealth of the family, but they will always be lavish in relation to the family's means, sometimes representing close to the family's entire income for a year. In some cases the young men will be presented with cars, television sets, radios, their own beds (something of a luxury, matting being a more common sleeping base) and other pieces of furniture. Other young men will be given far more modest tokens, but usually the presentations include some form of livestock; these will soon enough be needed to pay the bridal price or lobola. Another constant is a Western-style suit, in which the young man is expected, by custom, to get married, and which, for this reason, is often bought a size ot two too large for immediate use.

As the time draws ever nearer, feasts are prepared at home to celebrate the attainment of manhood by the *abakwetha*, and the presents that are to be given are put out on public display.

In the bush the camps that have housed the initiates for three months are burnt, along with the blanket and garments the youths have worn during their isolation. And at girls secluded at the same time in any particular village. The initiation is embarked upon after the girl's first menstruation but needs to be completed before she becomes sexually active; should she fall pregnant before the seclusion, she will be ostracized and her children will be treated as outcasts.

In the older and more traditional context – still practised in some places – the period of seclusion is three months in duration. In this form the first two months are spent essentially in preparation. The girl is prohibited from any communication with men and is bound in other ways to the initiation process: she is being instructed by her mother and other older women, and on two occasions is taken to the river for ceremonial cleansing. In essence, though, for these two months she is merely in a kind of bridging state between normal life and the ritual time of the initiation.

In the modern context, with the girls having to stay out of school during the time of seclusion and life no longer being organized around ritual, the process is pared down to its minimum. That minimum, the month-long seclusion, is common in all its features between both variants; thus there is no need to refer to the older form by way of distinction again.

The female initiation begins at full moon and with a symbolic return to the state of nature. The girl is stripped naked on the morning of the appointed day – usually a Friday – and from this moment on she is to avoid all contact with males. During the course of that day her head, eyebrows and pubic hair are shaved, while she sits in a corner attended by the older girls who will serve as her guides. A curious musical instrument is produced – these days an open tin drum stretched over with elastic bands, to produce weird twanging sounds – and to the accompaniment of this, songs are sung.

This goes on until evening, when the girls gather around a campfire – the guides naked and the girls undergoing the initiation wrapped in their blankets. First they sing songs, then as the night progresses, they launch into an orgy of licensed abuse against the male sex and against women who have failed to undergo the appropriate initiation procedures. A special stock of sticks is kept at hand to beat men or uninitiated females who may intrude on the ceremony.

According to informants the brunt of their cursing is directed against the bodies of men and the organs of their masculinity, but at the same time the cursing ritual serves as a somewhat perverse celebration of the sexual power of women. Much is made of the need of the men for the 'thing you cannot have'. Behaviour on this night may go to any extremes. (Informants told us that the girls on this night often go to the side of the road, and, as cars pass will lift their clothes to flaunt their unattainable bodies.)

At the end of the night, having danced and cursed themselves out, the girls go down to the river. Here the initiate is ritually washed before being returned to her homestead. The next day, a celebration is held at her home and at the end of this she is again ceremonially washed before being removed to the specially constructed room where she will spend her seclusion.

From this moment on, her only human contact will be with women. Among these are the grandmothers or *gogos* of the village who come at irregular intervals to share with her the lore of the tribe. Much of what they say is couched in fable (in which the major players are usually animals), but their intervention also includes more practical instruction. They and the mother, at least in the more traditional context, instruct the girl in the arts of traditional architecture and beadworking. Like many other institutions of

BELOW: *Stores of food for an Ndebele initiation feast at Weltevrede village in Kwa-Ndebele (see also following pages).*

Ndebele culture, though, this one has lapsed alarmingly in recent years and, so informants said, it is relatively rare to find a girl being thus instructed these days.

Mainly, the girl is in training to become a homemaker and matriarch. Throughout the seclusion she is expected to be practising her home maintenance skills: washing, cleaning, sweeping, dusting, scraping dung over cracked walls, and so on. Her role is somewhat like that of an elf in a fairy story; since she is to be isolated during this period, she does her work in the family home early in the morning or late at night, when there is nobody around to see her.

At the end of the month of her seclusion, the girl, now a woman, is ready to 'come out' in a ceremony that marks the conclusion of the initiation ritual. She is taken to the river for a final ceremonial washing; the clothes she has worn during her seclusion are burnt to symbolize the death of the girl she was, and she is presented with the stiff beaded apron, the *isiphephetu* (usually made by her mother or grandmother), which symbolizes her ascent from childhood to womanhood.

As is the case with the male initiation, the changed status of the girl is celebrated with feasting at the home of each girl who has undergone the initiation within the community in succession, but here there is a difference. The round of feasting to celebrate the girls' coming out also serves as a marriage market.

As they move from feast to feast, the girls – now dressed in *isiphephetu* and encased in such a profusion of beaded hoops (*golwani*) on their necks, legs and arms as to closely resemble the Michelin man – line up before the male guests at the feasts.

Around their necks they are wearing tambooti necklaces – made from small rectangles of carved wood strung together with brightly coloured and, these days, usually plastic beads and various charms. 'Tambooti' are associated with none of the more enduring tribal virtues. With the rich dark smell of the tambooti wood and the fripperies surrounding them, the necklaces are merely tokens of flirtatiousness. Along with the tambooti, and often worked into its frivolous conglomerations, the girls wear a whistle, and each in turn uses this to draw attention to

OPPOSITE: *At the commencement of the seclusion that constitutes the female initiation, a feast is held where older girls sing the praises of the girl undergoing the initiation – and show themselves off to potential husbands.*
BOTTOM LEFT: *Matrons arriving at another of the several female initiation parties we attended in the Weltevrede area.*
BOTTOM MIDDLE AND BELOW: *Like most aspects of Ndebele culture, initiation parties are susceptible to regional and local variations in such matters as the blankets worn and the presence or absence of accessories like headgear, dark glasses and the like. The picture at bottom middle was taken on the farm Ongesiens, near Middelburg; the one below was taken at the Weltevrede initiation party featured on pages 41-42.*

herself, then ululates and dances – as far as dancing is possible in the armour of hoops she is wearing – while the men admire and assess her charms.

Often they will make an offer of lobola (a marriage price or dowry) to the father there and then. Such lobola varies from place to place and from trade-off to trade-off, but a fairly typical price for a wife would be around R1 500 in cash or five cows and R500.

Despite this parade for the benefit of the men, their role remains limited. They sit to one side under a tree, usually in special structures something like children's playpens. Here they drink beer, they are served courses of food and, as often as not, as the day goes on, they indulge in increasingly frenetic, raucous and unsteady bouts of dancing, accompanied by clapping and vocal improvisation.

As is the case with most of the Ndebele celebrations, the ritual belongs to the women. In the modern context, however, the celebrations of initiation stand as practically the only time that women still appear in the full spendour of their traditional regalia. Here you will see women wearing *dzilla* – though usually of the plastic, clip-on variety – along with decorated festive headgear, marriage blankets, *golwani*, the beaded aprons (the *ijogolo* of the married woman, the *iziphephetu* of the initiated girls and the *lighabi* of the younger girls).

An astonishing and exotic spectacle they make too. It is here on an occasion such as this – with the older women regal and stiff, the girls tinkling and shimmering as they dance, the recent initiates armoured in *golwani* – that one catches a glimpse of just how extraordinary such events must have been in the past. Perhaps more than this, one senses how powerful the visual expression of tribal pride and tribal difference must once have been made.

## POMETS

Initiation festivities are overseen by a designated woman from the village whose role is perhaps best described as being that of a traditional policeman. Her function is in part to maintain decorum and to see to it that the proper order of things is observed.

Mainly she ensures that the women are appropriately attired according to custom, and if they are not she imposes 'fines'. Sometimes these are in the form of cash payments, or payments in kind. Mostly, however, the penalties are extracted in dances: the offender is required to dance without the usual accompaniment of clapping and ululation, and often to choruses of derision, for a period specified by this officer, before her offence against tradition is forgiven.

Though of course the business of sustaining tradition has its serious side, the practices referred to above have a lighthearted and humorous vocabulary and material culture associated with them. Thus the arbiter of Ndebele taste is referred to as a 'traffic officer' or 'Code 10 Driver' (in reference to the qualification needed to drive ultraheavy duty vehicles on the roads).

In order to earn this status within the game, the traffic officer must possess an item variously known as an 'ID', a 'driver's licence' and a 'pomet'. The latter is a bastardization of the word 'permit', and it registers the woman's status within the traditional structures of the tribe. Though the details of the ceremony remain unclear, such a pomet is awarded to a woman whose degree of possession in the dance and whose punctiliousness in traditional observance are judged particularly pleasing to the ancestors. Such a pomet serves as a traditional diploma of the highest order. Armed with it, whether she is officiating or not, she is (if she is Ndzundza) entitled to participate in any traditional gathering in Ndzundza territory. The pomet also establishes her as 'chief traffic officer' at traditional gatherings in her own area.

The pomet was originally an item of beadwork, often bearing numbers and words as visible proof of driver status within the community, but latterly the form of this item has changed significantly. Nowadays it is usually a kind of wallhanging, with a grass mat for a base and various details – often words, beaded or embroidered on the surface – as well as bits of beading affixed. And though it might look like a purely decorative item the pomet is, as explained above, an object potently charged with traditional significances.

During our research and wanderings, we attended one ceremony, held on the farm Ongesiens in celebration of the coming out of an initiated girl. Here nobody was dressed in tribal regalia, excepting the girls who had been part of the initiation rites. For the rest, the women were clad in a motley assortment of old-style Western party clothes and modern fashions.

When I asked the reason for this lack of traditional observance, the traffic officer was pointed out to me as being as innocent of characteristically Ndebele adornment as anybody else there. Unless the traffic officer observed the tradition, it was explained, nobody else was obliged to. And, the informant confided, it was only when visitors were expected that the traffic officer these days felt the need to observe the old customs; since we had arrived unexpectedly, we had caught them in informal mode and unprepared. Even the chief traffic officer, in these times of change, drives on the wrong side of the road!

BELOW AND OPPOSITE: *Examples of the pomet or 'Driver's Licence', which establishes the owner's credentials as a matron of standing in the community. The beaded item (opposite, bottom) is made to be worn in the manner shown below – where the notion of 'Police' establishes the standing of the wearer in the community. The other two pictures opposite show pomets made to be kept at home rather than worn. The example at top left is a contemporary version of the beaded item featured at top right.*

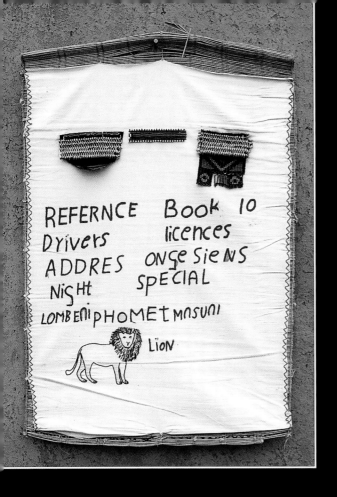

REFERNCE  Book 10
Drivers  licences
ADDRES  ONGESieNS
NiSHt  SPECIAL
LOMBENi PHOMET MNSUNI
Lion

# CHAPTER 3

# MURAL ART

*Far from being timelessly 'traditional', Ndebele wallpainting has its roots only in the 1940s.*
*Though almost from the start it has had a strongly commercial aspect, it nevertheless flowered*
*rapidly through a succession of styles to become one of the glories of Ndebele culture*
*and one of its most distinctive assertions of tribal identity.*

ABOVE: *Particularly in the KwaNdebele villages, wallpainting is done mostly with commercially available paints. But the Ndebele women often use them in combinations that make the colours all their own.*

OPPOSITE: *Wallpainter Francina Ndimande at work. Unlike most Ndebele painters, Francina is constantly at work, changing, improving and redesigning the decoration on her walls. In part, it is because she believes it pleases the ancestors and protects the household from evil forces. Like Esther Mahlangu and others, Francina also makes a living from her painting.*

I t might come as something of a shock to ethnic purists that the styles of Ndebele wallpainting that we identify as 'traditional' have their beginnings barely half a century ago. The first 'Ndebele-style' wallpaintings that we know of were photographed by Pretoria architect and university academic A L Meiring at a single settlement in the Hartebeestfontein area during the late 1940s – and there is every indication that it was in fact here that the practice of decorative and geometric wallpainting, at least as we think of it today, had its origins among the Ndebele. Photographing Ndebele dress and material culture barely a decade earlier, Alfred Duggan-Cronin recorded no such home decoration in the areas he visited. Nor is it mentioned in any of the other sources from earlier in the century, despite the relative proximity of the Ndzundza to white settlements after the indenture of the nation.

For all that, the style is not without its antecedents, and there is evidence of specimens of Ndebele wall decoration that predate the 1940s. Certain elderly women told us that they had learnt to mix earth pigments as children – mainly ochres, ranging from browns to a startling yellow – and that such earth pigments had routinely been used along with charcoal as coverings for walls. Even today, in many areas, such earth powders, along with pinks and mauves obtained from crushing stones, are often used to decorate walls – usually in conjunction with commercial PVAs and whitewash. Though almost certainly the ochres and charcoal were employed prior to the 1940s, no record

exists to show whether the other colours were put to this kind of use, or in what ways they were specifically used. Some clue, however, might be gleaned from the ways in which many Ndzundza who have remained on the farms of whites since the defeat of the Ndebele in 1883 – and who have therefore been relatively cut off from the history of Ndebele settlements – continue to decorate their homes: often with a medley of monochrome coats of earth pigment, sometimes bordered at the edges and around door and window frames with charcoal or contrasting hues.

The second of the antecedents is a form of decoration which, so informants claim, has been practised for hundreds of years. Here the design is executed by dragging the fingers through a wet plaster, usually cow dung, to leave a variety of possible markings, from straight parallels or basic geometries, to repeated squiggles and wave patterns. Such designs – generally, though certainly erroneously, referred to as representing 'tyre tracks' – appear to have a history that goes back further than any reliable record of Ndebele material culture, for those painters who remember the birth of the modern wallpainting techniques attest that they were taught the finger painting style by their mothers around the time of initiation.

In truth, it is unlikely that the practice of finger painting on walls by the Ndebele goes back much further than the middle of the nineteenth century. The reason for this, as is discussed later in chapter four, is that, as far as there is evidence, the Ndebele lived in grass huts before that time. However, with the ravages wrought during the

Difaqane, significant admixture occurred between the Ndebele and their Sotho and Pedi neighbours, which resulted in the Ndebele switching from grass to mud walls in the construction of their huts and integrating in their cultural life the originally Sotho practice of decorating those walls with finger painting.

Many informants also point to another important distinction between the older finger painting technique and the later wallpainting tradition. According to a number of women, particularly from the more backward-looking Nebo district, it is only the patterns derived from the finger painting style that have any real sacred significance. In terms defined by the Ndebele belief system, these are the decorative practices demanded by the ancestors as part of the culture of continuity. Some – mostly from the Nebo district – went so far as to claim that sickness and misfortune would inevitably result were these designs not present on their walls for the ancestors to see.

By contrast with these spiritually loaded motifs, the explosion of geometric colour most usually associated with Ndebele wallpainting is essentially profane and, so the painters themselves never tired of insisting, merely 'decorative'. It is this development that has its roots in the Hartebeestfontein settlement. Why and how the practice of the brightly coloured, quasi-representational and geometric wallpainting we identify as 'Ndebele' should have emerged there and then is a matter for speculation, but at least part of the answer might lie in the history of the Hartebeestfontein settlement.

Before the defeat of the Ndzundza at Mapoch's Caves in 1883, the royal heir Fene, along with his advisors, had managed to escape to Hartebeestfontein, where he was joined in 1899 by the Ndzundza regent, Nyabela. Thus, though in terribly reduced form, some kind of continuity of Ndzundza authority structures was maintained, and in 1888 at the termination of the Ndebele indenture, it was to this place that many of the Ndzundza migrated. In 1923, however, after the Ndzundza royalists had managed to scrape together enough money to buy land for their king at Weltevrede, those who remained at Hartebeestfontein found themselves yet again in exile from the symbols of their tribal identity.

With this as background, the way that most observers have interpreted the sudden flowering of wallpainting is as a visible assertion of that identity. Cut off from the embodiment of their group identity – the king and the ritual functionaries who surrounded him – the Ndzundza Ndebele are thought to have experienced some kind of need, conscious or unconscious, to materially express their Ndebeleness and to distinguish themselves from the groups surrounding them. In this group psychology, so the theory would have it, the whole tradition of wall-painting was born. Most forcefully put forward by Elizabeth Schneider in her doctoral thesis on Ndebele wallpainting, this interpretation is lent some credence by the Ndebele themselves. The stock explanation given by members of the tribal group is that wall decoration does indeed serve to set the Ndebele apart from their neigh-bours, and, as more than one informant put it, 'to tell the world there are Ndebele living here'.

If the cultural self-expression theory goes some of the way towards explaining the origins of Ndebele wallpaint-ing, then it needs to be balanced against other factors. With the publication of Meiring's photographs in 1955, public interest – specifically among whites – in the wall-painting of the Hartebeestfontein Ndzundzas grew rapid-ly. Other photographers, notably Constance Stuart Larrabee, and assorted consumers of the exotic had already by 1950 begun their own documentations of the Hartebeestfontein Ndzundza, and in time a busy little tourist industry grew up around the settlement – with significant economic benefits for the inhabitants.

The wallpainting of the Ndzundza responded like some hothouse plant. Less than a decade after it was first record-ed by Meiring – the painting style had already undergone a marked evolution. Where the earliest examples showed only the most simple and basic of decorative elements – outlined windows and door frames, edgings done in whitewash, and the occasional rudimentary geometric design executed in earth pigment and charcoal – by the mid 1950s, the designs had evolved spectacularly. Distinctive motifs such as the 'razor blade' and the step design were in evidence, and the abstractions from domes-tic imagery that even today characterize the painting of the Ndebele had already been essayed on the walls of the Hartebeestfontien settlement.

In some ways, it is not surprising that the style should have matured so quickly. The women of the settlement had available a reservoir of imagery to draw from in the quasi-representational styles that in recent decades had come to the fore in their traditional beadwork. It was indeed to this that they looked initially for the imagery to reproduce on their walls, borrowing the stylized represen-tations of huts and kraals as well as the more mysterious symbols, such as the triangular shape which Ndzundza respondents described as an 'axe head' – the curious sym-bol that later adapted as the electric light.

Soon enough, though, this relationship was to be, if not reversed, at least made more cross-referential. The greater flexibility of the painting medium – particularly as

commercial paints came to supplement the earth pig-ments with which the Hartebeestfontein women had started out – allowed for and even predicted a rapid expansion of the artistic vocabulary of the beadwork. It was not long before the imagery migrated in a full circle, with the 1960s style in beadwork taking its cue largely from innovations in wallpainting. To give one example, the so-called 'Ufly', or aeroplane, which became relatively common in beadworking around this time, has, as far as can be ascertained, its origins in wallpainting.

Such developments, however, only occurred with the passage of time. In the early 1950s the possibilities of wall-painting were only beginning to emerge, and its practice was more or less restricted to the Hartebeestfontein dis-trict. It took another outside intervention before decora-tive wallpainting really began to establish itself fully as an Ndebele 'tradition'. Let us sketch in a little background at this point.

Meiring, the Pretoria architect who discovered the wall-painting at Hartebeestfontein, was, at the same time as being much interested in the material culture of Africa, an enthusiastic supporter of the then newly installed Afrikaner National Party government, and his vision of Africa was strongly coloured by its ideologies. Notably, Meiring's interest in the Hartebeestfontein settlement was inextricably tied up with his espousal of National Party policies of separate development. Here was a triumphant

OPPOSITE AND BELOW: *The oldest technique of wall decoration among the Ndebele is exe-cuted by dragging the fingers through a mud and dung plaster applied to the walls to leave rhythmic patterning. Properly known as* kguphu, *the designs are more commonly referred to as 'tyre tracks'. While most Ndebele wallpainting is essentially unmagical in char-acter, these designs are believed to protect the household from malevolent spirits.*

PAGES 50-51: *Especially in the more rural areas, the Ndebele still use earth pigments to colour their walls. The browns, pinks and ochres are obtained by grinding stones; the black is derived from battery cells or charcoal, and the sky-blue is often a mixture of washing blue and whitewash. Frequently, these nat-ural products are used in combination with commercial paints, as seen in the detail on page 51.*

PAGES 52-59: *These photographs were taken at two specially constructed tourist villages: Botshabelo outside Middelburg and the KwaNdebele Tourism Board's 'Traditional Village' in the Bronkhorstspruit district. They serve as some kind of record of the range of styles which have emanated from the Ndebele wallpainting tradition, many of which have disappeared from actual villages. Traditional dress, as worn in the tourist villages, disappeared from the everyday context long before such decorative wallpainting began.*

example of an ethnic grouping expressing, preserving, adapting its own culture and 'tradition' in parallel with the evolution of the other 'peoples' of South Africa and in defiance of the melting pot of post-colonial history. It must have seemed a heaven-sent illustration of the separatist philosophy of ethno-history which underpinned the government's policies of apartheid, and Meiring was not slow in promoting it as such.

When the death of the owner of the Hartebeestfontein farm placed the future of the Ndzundza settlement under threat, Meiring, in liaison with the government's tourist authority, succeeded in having the entire hamlet moved to a new site north-west of Pretoria, in territory later to be

designated part of the Bophuthatswana homeland. The new settlement, called KwaMsiza (after the then leader of the community) was overtly established with the purpose of functioning as a 'tourist village', and, in pursuit of this goal, was fulsomely poeticized and promoted in publicity material as a 'traditional Ndebele village'.

This, of course, it was not – not by any stretch of the imagination. But if the whole process of its establishment was underpinned by ironies, the final irony is at the expense of those who would be outraged by the fiction that was written at KwaMsiza. The village did indeed swiftly become a prime example of the form and appearance of the typical Ndebele settlement, but this happened in reverse of the expectable order as women from other settlements and villages emulated the pioneering wallpainting styles that emerged first at Hartebeestfontein and later at the tourist village.

Undoubtedly, part of the motivation behind the rapid spread of the wallpainting style was of a commercial order, with the kinsfolk of the Hartebeestfontein Ndzundzas seeking to share in the cultural windfall. Even today, there is a basic expectation that visitors to the villages of the Ndebele will pay for their aesthetic enrichment. As often as not, a tour of the painted homestead will be preceded

PAGES 54-55 AND ABOVE: *According to the chronology presented at Botshabelo, the criss-cross design on page 54 is a forerunner to the razor-blade motif or* umetsho *featured on page 55 and above. Such linear chronologies, however, are dangerous; the differences in style tend to be regional far more than historical.*

by negotiations of varying degrees of complexity around the cash value of the experience to the tourist. Some Ndebele will charge by the photograph; others, like the well-known wallpainter Esther Mahlangu, will demand payment on top of the basic rate for such services as interviews and explanations.

It is a refreshingly frank sense of exchange that informs dealings with the Ndebele, but it is worth noting that it stands in marked and pointed contrast with the way one deals as a visitor in most rural communities in South Africa. In these, according to African usage, it is more customary for the visitor to be honoured with a gift than for him or her to be expected to give one. But then – and this is the point – the visitor is not going to the Ndebele as a guest but as a customer; that is implicit in the history of wallpainting as an Ndebele tradition.

If, however, Ndebele wallpainting has always constituted something of an industry, it is not to imply that this is the only reason for the Ndebele decorating their walls. One should be no more inclined to think this than to

attribute the Sistine Chapel ceiling to Michaelangelo's patronage by the Church. Whatever the initial impetus behind the spread of painting styles among the Ndebele, the practice was rapidly assimilated within the culture at large. Taking the Hartebeestfontein and KwaMsiza styles as the starting point, the matrons of the Ndebele rapidly made the practice of wallpainting their own, and it was not only in those specific places but throughout the territory occupied by the Ndebele that the style was refined and brought to full articulation. By the 1960s geometrically painted walls were instantly recognizable as Ndebele attributes – as distinctive as the dzilla or the tribe's particular marriage beadwork – and came to constitute an important part of the cultural self-expression of the people.

Thus, although, as noted above, few of the Ndebele would view wallpainting as possessing any sacred significance, it nevertheless quickly became integrated into the ritual structures of the tribe. Though the observance, like so many others, is lapsing today, the male initiation or wela became the occasion for either painting or renewing wall decoration, and its completion would always coincide with the family celebrations and ceremonies that mark the culmination of the initiation rites.

Of greater importance, though, is the more general role that wallpainting came to play in an area of material culture that is of prime spiritual importance for the women of the Ndebele: the celebration of the domestic environment. Within the traditional value system, Ndebele women are as much mystically bound to the home as they are practically. As is discussed in chapter five, their beadwork consists primarily of a set of charms associated with the home and the family. Even the space of the homestead is shot through with mystical and magical meanings, and there are taboos associated with certain thresholds within the homestead. Thus, for instance, children may not cross the thresholds to certain courtyards while ceremonies are being enacted. Similarly, on ritual occasions at least, men are forbidden from entering spaces reserved for women.

The way that the majority of Ndebele women interpreted and brought to full articulation the new, decorative wallpainting styles was to transpose all the domestic imagery to the walls of their homes. Ndebele wallpainting at its most basic generally reproduces the concerns and motifs of the beadwork but, partly because of the greater flexibility of the medium and partly because the artists were not bound to the same extent by custom, the walls allowed for more liberated explorations.

Beginning with fairly rudimentary geometric designs on broad planes of colour, as pioneered at Hartebeestfontein and KwaMsiza, the wall decoration of the Ndebele rapidly grew more linear and more complex in its articulation. More and more of the background came to be filled in, and in ever increasing detail until figure and ground came to be integrated into an all-over patterned effect. By the 1970s the style had developed into the intricate stylization made famous by such artists as Esther Mahlangu and

BELOW: *An aerial view of an Ndebele tourist village near Bronkhorstspruit.*
PAGES 58-59: *These designs are descriptive of the modern period – according to the chronology presented at the tourist villages anyway. In fact, such designs are relatively uncommon outside of the former KwaNdebele homeland.*

ABOVE AND TOP RIGHT: *Two details from the walls of Esther Mahlangu's homestead in Weltevrede. The image on the left is derived, with variations, from a beadworking design. On the right is an example of a recent move towards figuration in her work – this one taken from the decoration on her garage door, which serves as a kind of hoarding for passing motorists.*

Francina Ndimande, and subsequently has altered yet further to occasionally include organic representational details: figures, animals, and the like. In recent years, even a painter like Esther Mahlangu has begun experimenting with stylized Ndebele figures, ironically drawn as much from the white painter Alexis Preller as they are from life or from tradition.

Ndebele wallpainting has, since its beginnings, always been in flux, but attempts to chronologize it are doomed to failure. While a relatively coherent history was evident until the 1950s around Hartebeestfontein and KwaMsiza, various kinds of styles have always co-existed. Even today, decoration reminiscent of the earliest examples of the form are as common throughout the territory of the Ndebele as is the fully elaborated style of such painters as Esther Mahlangu.

Ndebele women decorating their walls may have had, so to speak, one foot in the past of their beadworking traditions, but the other was always in the colonial and post-colonial world into which their history was dragging them. From the early geometric and essentially purely decorative designs, they evolved a language of domestic imagery that reflects a kind of interface between the world of the cities and the rural outposts where it was produced.

Many writers on the subject have commented on the fact that Ndebele women, on returning to their rural homes from the cities – where for the most part they worked as domestic servants in white households – chose to reproduce on the walls of their own homes details drawn from the homes of their employers. The classic example here is that of the electric light which, since the 1950s, has featured prominently as a motif in wallpainting. But it is by no means the only one. Telephone poles, though less frequently to be found in wallpainting, are just as symbolically eloquent in places where there is, still, not a telephone for miles. Many Ndebele wallpaintings show multistorey houses such as only the very wealthy, even today, actually own. We find swimming pools, staircases, blocks of flats, industrial-type structures, even such details as hot and cold taps drawn on a house set some hundreds of metres away from a communal water point in the KwaNdebele village of Waterval B.

There is something immeasurably poignant about all of this – the walls of these homesteads bearing testimony to the aspirations of their owners, appropriating in picture form the things which the condition of their lives has denied them. It is like trying to take a bite out of an advertisement for a hamburger.

Some of the women we spoke to were quite explicit about this aspect of their work. One of many, named Sophie Mahlangu (this one from Wolwekraal), had decorated her home with, among other things, a foursquare house with windows, a white door and a verandah.

Protruding at an angle from the walls of the (represented) house, there were two balanced arrow shapes. Referring to these Sophie Mahlangu observed they were the chimneys from an invisible stove. Her own house, like many Ndebele homes boasted no such refinements; cooking was done in the time-honoured way, in a specially prepared depression in the floor of the cooking hut.

'You can't see the stove, even though it is there,' Sophie says. 'Rich people have stoves and they have chimneys and they have living rooms and patios. These are beautiful things and I want them for myself. That is why I paint them on my walls.'

Moving around the house, we went through the same routine in relation to the electric lights with which she had seen fit to decorate many of her walls, then the squares of green she depicted as growing from the bases of doors and representing lawns, then the multiple rooms that she described as existing inside the simple shapes she had actually represented.

BELOW: *The use of decorative painting on interior walls is uncommon among the Ndebele, many of whom explain the impulse behind their art in terms of 'telling the world that Ndebeles are living here'.*
PAGES 62-63: *Page 62 depicts three variations of the* umetsho *or razor-blade design. The top image is from the homestead of Francina Ndimande, the bottom two are from that of Esther Mahlangu. Page 63 portrays some of the variety of figurative images that are sometimes interspersed with geometric design on Ndebele walls.*

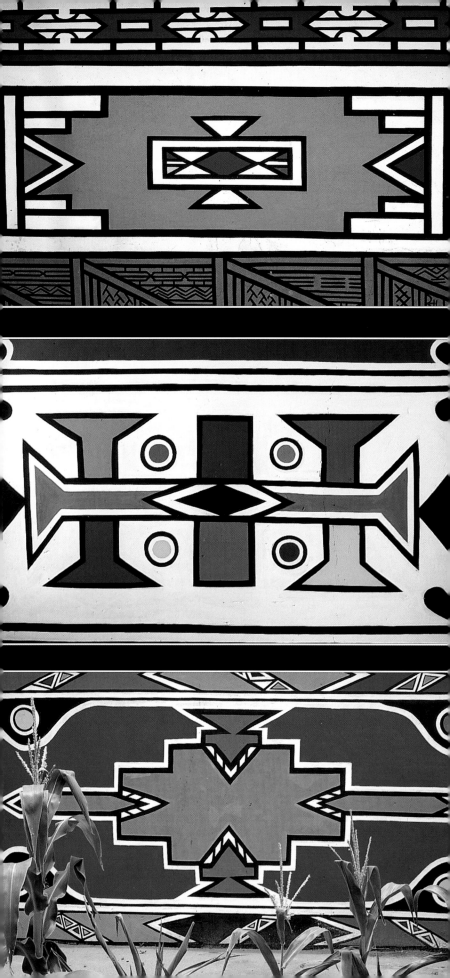

'I want it to be beautiful,' she concludes. 'Like a real house with all of these things. It's like having a house with these things.'

I use Sophie Mahlangu as a more or less random example; any number of other women expressed much the same sense of aspiration in talking about their choice of such relatively upmarket motifs in their wallpainting. But perhaps the most poignant version was given by Martha Ndala who said of her rendering of an electric light: 'I gave it to the house because the house doesn't have lights.'

Without wishing to overemphasize this aspect of wall decoration, there is certainly an element of sympathetic magic operating at some level here, a kind of appropriation through symbolism, but such issues are inescapably nebulous, and the distinction between illustrating something out of liking and fascination and vicarious ownership is always difficult to define. Suffice to say, the choice of subject matter is characteristically dealt with in light and humorous ways when the Ndebele wallpainters talk about it themselves. The primary impulse is decorative, they insist.

Let us then look at the wallpainting in decorative terms. What is particularly striking here are the relationships between representational elements and abstract geometries; the way in which those motifs that have been employed in the decoration are integrated into the overall design. It is particularly this tension between the representational and the geometrical that gives modern Ndebele wallpainting its singular character. In the most complex of the paintings, motifs are never just representational elements; like the old woman who becomes a young girl in the optical conundrum, they shift between being depictions and being abstract elements of an overriding design. In the same process, and guided by the differences in colour value, they move between two and three dimensions in the viewing, thus generating a peculiarly active and dynamic kind of visual field.

Speaking here as an art critic, let me say that the best of the wallpaintings represent a sophisticated distillation of sensory experience and a visually articulate approach to making art. Though they come from a very different psychic place (and without wanting to subsume the techniques within a Western sense of art) they share a number of stylistic features with European Cubism. Indeed, the guiding principles behind Ndebele wallpainting have a lot in common with European Cubism.

In Cubism, part of the project is to look at things not from a single and static viewpoint but in terms of a multiplicity of different but connected moments of perception. The idea is that by fusing together a variety of aspects of

experience, fuller, more complex and less expectable versions can be created of its objects. Objects are seen from all sides at once; they are, so to speak, folded out within the two dimensions of the design. A very similar kind of approach can often be discerned in Ndebele wallpainting. By way of example, let us look at a typical section of one of the walls at the homestead of Francina Ndimande.

The basic subject matter is, predictably enough, that of a house, and on either side of it there are zigzag patterns bordering planes of colour and, protruding from the roof, stylized depictions of electric lights. Now, pressed for an explanation of the zigzag patterns, the artist explains that they represent staircases.

'Where do they lead?' I ask, the stairs being placed against the walls.

'Actually, they are inside the house,' Francina Ndimande explains. 'I have put them outside so you can see them. You couldn't see them if they were on the inside.'

In similar vein, a design made up of a cross inside a rectangle was identified by other artists as a fireplace, while chevrons at the edge of a wall were described as representing a fence, and so on.

A similarly liberated attitude can be discerned in the way colour planes are used. Often, should the design

OPPOSITE AND LEFT: *Many of the motifs used by Ndebele wallpainters can be read as a record of aspiration. Thus, the motif of the electric light is usually explained by the phrase 'because we don't have them'. In similar vein the 'Ufly' or aircraft was often explained in terms of travelling to far-off lands where there was no racial discrimination.*

PAGES 66-67: *Details from the walls of Margaret Skosana's homestead in Pieterskraal village. The urban imagery, the painter said, derives from a period when she worked as a domestic servant in the city. The way she integrates details such as churches, flatblocks, clocks and electric lights into a planar geometry, however, is unique.*

expressively the transformations that were occurring within the culture. One of the most poignant illustrations to be found of this very abstract process is in the way that letters and numbers are used in Ndebele wallpainting. Over the past decade, with the spread of basic literacy, it has not been uncommon for Ndebele artists to include within their designs, the clan name of the resident family, or the block number of the house. Such symbols are, however, usually used outside of language and symbol systems, purely for their visual properties – and for the empowering learning that they represent to the functionally illiterate. The number '2', for example, is a particular favourite among Ndebele wallpainters; when asked why they deploy it in their designs, they say either that they would like to be able to read, or simply that they like the way the back of the digit bends on its way to the horizontal plane.

Often though the process appears to work in reverse – with the meaning of Western symbols being taken over but the form being significantly altered. In this way an irregular and ungeometric form painted on a wall in yellow might be identified as representing a stop sign. A row of black dots might designate a highway, an inverted cone painted in black a garden of trees.

To return to Francina Ndimande's house, the 'steps', while representing a staircase, also hark back to older stylizations in Ndebele beadworking. Several older informants said that as young girls being instructed in beading, they had been shown a particular formula for representing houses. It had stepped walls and a sort of truncated triangle on top. Now, in elaborating the same step design to represent staircases, wallpainters like Francina Ndimande are adapting old formulas to newer concerns. But at the same time they are creating continuities between the older world of tradition and the new world which has been irrevocably changed by the presence of the whites.

If we think about art as a set of practices in culture which work with the raw date of perception, filtering and interpreting those data and rendering them as coded versions of experience, then the art of Ndebele wallpainting becomes perhaps easier to comprehend. It is above all a form which mediates between the culturally 'inner' world of tradition and the 'outer' world of dominant Western technologies. It is in a state of constantly becoming, held in a tension between abstraction and representation or, if you like, between possibility of the geometric mark and the actuality of the motif. In this way it becomes a kind of ritualized working through of the historical condition of its practitioners, a way for the Ndebele of simultaneously assimilating and appropriating in consciousness a brave, if threatening, new world.

demand it, you will see a two-dimensional rectangle or triangle of green (or some other colour) appended at the base of a house motif. This will be explained as showing the garden. Its flowers, though, may be placed elsewhere in the painting – for instance, on the roof, in response to the balances of the design.

The pictorial logic, then, is not of a rational or Cartesian order. Though they do retain some representational reference, the elements of the picture are freed from their immediate functions and float free as elements within the design. It is as though in Ndebele wallpainting everything is in a constant state of becoming, not of 'givenness'. As one informant put it: 'The house on the wall is not complete.'

This notion of the 'not complete' is one which gives profound access to the way that the painting functions. Precisely because it is such a new means of expression, Ndebele wallpainting has lent itself to the expression of the changing nature of Ndebele culture. It has – and has always had – one pole of reference which is specifically African, rooted in the spiritual beliefs of the Ndebele people. However, this art form emerged at a time when the Ndebele were oppressed and marginalized – but nonetheless influenced – by the culture of the West. Thus, wallpainting served just as strongly, through its imagery and its deeper concerns, to link the Ndebele with the new world in which they found themselves and so to mediate

# CHAPTER 4

# THE HOMESTEAD

*In Ndebele society, the homestead is more than just a living space; it reflects at the
same time relations with both other people and with the world of the ancestors. Re-establishing
the homestead in the middle decades of this century was a key element in the rebuilding
of the culture and in the flowering of Ndebele art.*

ABOVE AND OPPOSITE: *The earliest examples
of Ndebele wall decoration are those recorded
in the Hartebeestfontein area in the late
1940s by A L Meiring. These were of the type
illustrated above. Even today, especially in
rural areas, the majority of Ndebele homesteads are embellished by such simple contrasting lines and colours. As the photograph
opposite depicts, the effect, particularly in this
structural arrangement, can be very striking
and startlingly beautiful.*

On the farm Rietvallei in the Eastern Transvaal,
between present-day Belfast and Middelburg,
there is an excavation that has been dated back
more than three hundred years and which may be taken as
more or less typical of Ndebele architectural style prior to
the great southern African upheavals and migrations (the
Difaqane) of the early nineteenth century. It shows a series
of separate homesteads built around a central space which,
it is believed, marked an enclosure where the cattle
belonging to the resident community were penned.
Around this central space a series of circles mark the outer
borders of individual homesteads. Inside each of these are
the remains of a group of huts which once constituted a
homestead. In each case, there is one hut (measuring
between seven and eight metres in diameter) that is larger
than the others and that stands at the centre of the circle
defined by the other, smaller huts. According to the testimony of oral historians, the larger hut would have been
that occupied by the head of the household, while the
smaller huts orbiting, as it were, around it would have
housed his wives and children, or served as storerooms,
cooking spaces, and so on.

The huts themselves would have been made of grass
thatched over a framework of saplings. (Here, archaeologists have based their inferences on physical evidence as
well as on the memories contained in the oral tradition of
the Ndebele.) These saplings would have been fixed at
intervals within the circular trench defining the floor plan
of the hut, then either tied together at the top into a kind

of teepee form, or bent into a beehive shape, before being
covered over with thatch to provide both wall and roofing
in one continuous surface.

This design of this early Ndebele homestead is of interest to us for two reasons. One is that the basic building
style and design is generic to the Southern Bantu, and
more particularly, though with variations, was employed
by the subgroups of the South Nguni during the period
under consideration.

The other point of interest is that the seventeenth
century building methods differ markedly from Ndebele
practice today. The first phase of the change came some
decades after the Difaqane. With the ravages wrought in
that time of violent upheaval, the Southern Ndebele, like
most of their neighbours, were depleted and fragmented
by the 1830s, but under the leadership of their great
king, Mabhogo Mahlangu, as will be recalled from chapter one, the Ndzundza Ndebele had rebuilt their society
within a few decades in the area around the mountain
fortress (near today's Roossenekal) that came to be known
as Mapoch's Caves.

At Mapoch's Caves the Ndzundza were not the same
people they had been before. The Difaqane had changed
the face of the southern African hinterland more pro-
foundly than in the mere destruction of its kraals and
farmlands. Throughout the region, formerly powerful
polities had been reduced to straggling groups of refugees,
who, with survival pressing harder than custom, went
wherever they could find protection, regardless of any

ABOVE: *The reconstruction of a pre-Difaqane Ndebele hut at Botshabelo tourist village.*

above is in fact presented as the culmination of an earlier development in which the walls, though cylindrical and built around vertical poles, are surfaced with grasses. The structures featured at the Botshabelo village demonstrate a series of stages in the development of homestead construction, with the cylindrical walls growing taller in each successive example.

Be this as it may, the end result is the same. By the time the Boers broke the power of the Ndzundza in 1883, the characteristic architecture of the people had changed. When the Ndzundza set about constructing homes after their period of indenture they did so on the cone and cylinder model. They had also absorbed another custom from those Sotho who had become assimilated into the tribal stock: the practice of scratching decorative patterns on the walls of their homes, though the designs were different from those used by the Sotho. It was of course this wall patterning which, some 60 years after the period of indenture, was to lead to the explosion of decorative design that so excited the Pretoria architect A L Meiring.

But this is to get ahead. In the last years of the nineteenth century and the early years of the twentieth, the building of homes by the Ndzundza Ndebele was necessarily circumscribed and usually sporadic; they had, after all, no settled homes and for the most part were either little more than squatters or outright nomads. But where photographic documentation does exist, the house design that is shown until well into the 1930s, is that of the cone and cylinder. It is perhaps worth recording in this regard that by the early years of the twentieth century, the Manala subgroup, whose survivors were living among the Sotho at the Wallmansthal mission station, were similarly building on the cone and cylinder model – as is evidenced in photographs taken by the ethno-documentarist, Alfred Duggan-Cronin, during the 1930s.

Since the 1950s, however, with a strong Western influence again modifying the design of the Ndebele homestead, cone and cylinder construction has been the exception rather than the rule. Nevertheless, it is not unusual to see in the cluster of rectilinear buildings that make up a homestead, a single circular structure built on the cone and cylinder model, usually set somewhat back and constructed on a smaller scale than the rest of the buildings. There is some debate concerning the purpose of these structures, with some writers designating them as generic ancestral shrines. In our experience, however, and according to our informants, they always mark the presence of a sangoma within a household, though in some cases the sangoma had died and the building had been left standing in memoriam.

traditional enmities and differences. Thus it was that large numbers of particularly Sotho, but also Pedi, were taken in by the Ndzundza in the Roossenekal area. With the intermingling that resulted came not only genetic, but also social, cultural and political assimilation and, so to speak, an intercourse of tradition.

It was during this period that the Ndzundza began building in a different style. Borrowing from the Sotho, who were now part of their population, they moved away from the old Nguni beehive hut to a more adaptable form, that of the cone and cylinder. In this design, mud mixed with dung is packed around vertical poles set in a circle in the ground. The resulting cylinder is then fitted with rafters (in the form of a cone) and these are covered with grasses to create a thatched roof.

There are a number of variations on the basic theme. In the chronology of Ndebele living structures at Botshabelo tourist village near Middelburg, the design described

This circular room might loosely be described in one of its aspects as the sangoma's 'consulting room', as it is here that the sangoma treats those seeking remedies. It is also the place where herbal preparations and the paraphernalia of witchdoctoring are stored.

At the same time, it serves as a kind of omphalos for the ancestors, as they are believed to communicate most strongly with the sangoma in that place. Indeed, informants told us, they live under the ground of that sacred space; it is for this reason that visitors are required to remove their shoes before entering. Although not every sangoma's 'consulting room' that we encountered was built on the cone and cylinder model, the vast majority were – in pursuance of tradition, because, as the sangomas explained it, this is the way the ancestors demanded it. This exception aside, the characteristic domestic architecture of the Ndebele underwent a further transformation in

the 1940s and more particularly in the 1950s. Influenced by Western models the Ndebele gradually abandoned the cylinder in favour of the right-angled wall. As architect Peter Rich notes in his *Architecture of the Southern Ndebele*, besides the simple assimilation of new styles, there was also an element of practicality determining the change. Such items as window and door frames are typically manufactured for straight walls, and so too is the Western-style furniture that the Ndebele began to acquire as they grew more settled in a world dominated by Western goods and Western values. It was merely good sense to adapt with the times.

And the Ndebele have continued to adapt. At first the typical Ndebele homestead continued to be thatched, though the difference in design demanded different techniques. Nowadays, except in the white-owned farmlands and the impoverished and tradition-bound Nebo district,

BELOW: *An Ndebele homestead set within a Transvaal landscape on a white-owned farm. But the idyll is often illusory – conditions are harsh and for many Ndebele their life situation has barely changed since their indenture in the 1880s.*
PAGES 78-79: *Rural Ndebele homesteads. Beginning with a single core structure, in the traditional context, homesteads grow organically to accommodate the expanding family.*

ABOVE: *The exterior view of Francina
Ndimande's homestead in Weltevrede.*
RIGHT: *Esther Mahlangu in her parlour,
which reflects a curious mix of cultures:
Western-style furniture (still wrapped in its
protective plastic), distinctively Ndebele wallpainting, and curios brought back by the
artist from Paris and other world capitals she
has visited.*

in the face of powerfully directed attempts to break it was the re-establishment of the homestead. For Delius, and those who have followed him, this observation leads to the conclusion that the rebuilding of the homestead should be seen primarily as an act of political resistance.

Such an interpretation, however, while it certainly has validity, seems to take the point too far and would appear to confuse to some extent cause and effect. It makes more sense to stress the reassertion of an inherited tribal identity as the primary motivation, and the political resistance as something that follows from the context in which the gesture is made. In this interpretation, what is particularly important is the social dimension of the homestead.

More than mere living space, implicit in the homestead is a set of authority structures and a sense of order which constitutes its own justification. It is an order that rehearses in microcosm the structures and hierarchies of Ndebele society, embodying the distinctions between male and female, between young and old. Most importantly, perhaps, it enacts continuities, and it is a place that is inhabited not only by the living but also by the ancestral dead. To re-establish the token of such an order may well fly in the face of the oppressor, but it also serves internal needs within Ndzundza society.

thatched roofs are a rarity. More often the homesteads are roofed with uninsulated corrugated iron, which, though it might satisfy Ndebele aesthetic tastes and be far more convenient in the construction, leads to oven-like temperatures in the summer and nearly Arctic conditions in the winter months.

If the Ndebele homestead has looked to the present for its building techniques, its deeper form and its function are underwritten by tradition. Historian Peter Delius has demonstrated that, for the Ndzundza, one of the cruellest punishments imposed through indenture lay in the destruction of the family and its living unit, the homestead. Where formerly the Ndzundza had grouped together in extended family units, with the homestead often housing three generations of a line, the Boers respected (as far as they respected any kinship ties at all) only the right of the nuclear family to remain together. Thus the old homestead units came to be scattered in the indenture, their members finding themselves sometimes hundreds of miles away from one another.

Freed from the indenture, as recorded in chapter one, many Ndzundza attempted to regroup at places like Hartebeestfontein and to reinstate the old tribal authority structures. Part of the process of affirming tribal identity

Although one might assume that the will to return to the old social structure represented by the homestead was there from the beginning of the post-war period, the way was in actual fact some decades in coming. Among those Ndzundza who remained on white-owned farms the process was, for the most part, essentially organically achieved; as the once-indentured labourers had children and those children married and had children, so, with the passage of time, the homestead grew in complexity of its own accord. But for those among the Ndzundza who became displaced people on their release from indenture, first a place had to be found where they could settle, where they could put down roots and attempt to remake their society, both microcosmically and macrocosmically. This process took several decades, and although communities did develop at Hartebeestfontein, Kafferskraal and various other locations in the Transvaal, it was only with the purchase of the farm Weltevrede in 1923 and with the transfer of the other major branch of the Ndzundza to the Nebo district in 1938, that the beginnings of a permanent solution could be found. In fact it was, in general, only during the 1940s and the 1950s that a large-scale reassertion of the Ndebele homestead and of all that went with it really took place.

## THE MODERN HOMESTEAD

Regarding the order implicit in the structure of the Ndebele homestead, let us look in more detail at the ways in which that order is manifested. In common with the ancient, circular Nguni homestead design, the modern homestead is constructed around a central structure which tends to be larger than those subsequently erected. But it differs from the earliest designs in that where, as far as can be ascertained, the satellite huts were once positioned in a full circle around the central one, the modern design is more frontal, with the satellite structures being usually built to the side and in front of the larger central building. Only such service structures as cooking huts, storerooms and washing spaces are typically built these days to the back of the major structure. This central and defining structure serves as the living quarters of the head of the family, though it is essentially the domain of the wife. Not only does she traditionally design and build it, but if there is more than one wife, as is still sometimes the case in Ndebele society, each successive wife will build her own basic homestead, though usually on a reduced scale and in such a way as to integrate and interlock with the first.

The central structure is usually rectangular in shape, with the most common design having a central door, on

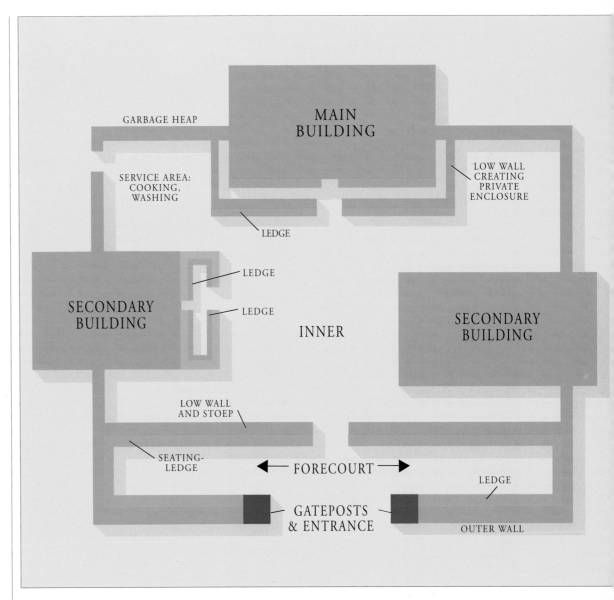

either side of which small, usually square framed windows are symmetrically set. Often the entrance is shaded by an overhang of roof, and characteristically it leads on to a mud-walled courtyard to the front.

With the core arrangement in place the next step in homestead design is to construct, to one side of the main building, a separate structure facing inwards, to give what researcher Elizabeth Schneider designates as an L-shape to the homestead as a whole. This second structure, often comprising a plurality of rooms and with its own courtyard, generally houses the children of the family – the boys and girls usually sleeping separately.

The next development tends to be a mirroring of the second construction on the opposite side of the courtyard, with the new buildings, similarly facing inwards, giving the whole a U-shape and creating an enclosed courtyard.

ABOVE: *The groundplan for a Ndebele homestead. While most of the features marked in the illustration are found in the majority of Ndebele homesteads, how they are arranged depends on individual circumstances.*

ABOVE AND OPPOSITE: *The gateposts of the traditional Ndebele homestead mark the boundary between the inside and the outside world. Thus, in such ornamented examples as Margaret Skosana's (above) in Pieterskraal they are decorated in the image of a homestead so as to convey this message to outsiders. The orbs which surmount the gateposts in this example and that featured on page 83 at top (Betty Mahlangu's homestead outside Middelburg), are described as representing lamps. Gabling is equally common and has probably also been borrowed from Western architecture.*

In the Platonic version of the Ndebele homestead, this basic design becomes repeatable. As a son grows up and marries, a house is constructed alongside the main dwelling at the base of the U, and with its own courtyard. As the son's family grows, his satellite homestead follows the same pattern of construction as the first, and so on. In reality, homesteads tend to be less structured, and fairly quickly lose Schneider's alphabetical neatness. Nevertheless, the principle of growth remains more or less discernible and available for analysis; it is a structuring of space and of living around age and position within the hierarchies of the family. It is significant in this regard that, at least within the more traditional context, when the parents of a family die, the structures in which they lived are not immediately demolished. They are left as reminders and as tokens of the continuity that links the living with the dead.

Such developments, of course, only occur over long periods. The basic homestead is built in the L- or U-shape, and as such, as noted above, it defines an interior courtyard. This courtyard, seen as a whole, ends in the outer retaining walls of the homestead, but it is usually subdivided into a series of minor courtyards, each defined by its own low walls and often stepped at different levels as well. Thus, coming in from the outer world through the gateposts, one enters first a forecourt. Moving towards the heart of the homestead, one comes to a second and sometimes a third and even a fourth minor courtyard.

Probably the easiest way to visualize this complexity of courtyards is to picture the groundplan of a very low-walled house which has been built without windows or a roof. And indeed it is very much like an exterior house, with each of the spaces accorded its own function – like rooms, though occupied according to more rigid social mores and hierarchies than is the case in a modern Western-style house.

It is essentially the women who 'own' the space of the courtyard, and it is here that they congregate and socialize, observing hierarchies based on age, station in life and social custom. Visitors are received in the forecourt, and it is a breach of etiquette to move beyond this area without invitation. In the inner courts, social as well as ceremonial activities take place, with a relatively strict hierarchy (according to age) determining who is allowed within which space. Thus, children generally remain in the outer spaces of the courtyard, young adults closer to the centre while the innermost spaces are reserved for the *igogo* (the grandmothers).

This, at least, is how it works in the traditional context. Like most traditional Ndebele observances, however, such hierarchies of space exist these days more in theory than in practice, and it is in fact relatively rare (except in the farmlands) to find the complex elaboration of spaces described above; more usually there is a forecourt and an inner court, and nothing more than that.

Despite the general breakdown of the old values and homesteading principles, there is one aspect of the Ndebele social organization of space which, to this day, is generally rigidly adhered to, particularly in what was KwaNdebele, and that is that men and women are seldom seen engaged in social activities with one another. While the women are almost always to be found within the confines of the homestead, busily keeping house, the men are almost always outside – usually in a shaded enclosure known as an *mtunzi*. In the old days the *mtunzi* was located near to the place where the man of the house kept his cattle and served to take him into his role as an animal husband. Nowadays, especially in the more developed areas of the former homeland, it is somewhere in the corner of the garden, and, in many cases at least, it is chiefly a place where the men while away their time socializing, listening to the radio and drinking. One cannot help thinking of it irreverently as a kind of a playpen for adults.

Such stereotyping may sound somewhat anachronistic, but for the Ndebele it is a crucial element of social organization. Thus it gives concrete form to the bonding of

BELOW: *The Ndebele homestead is above all the woman's domain. In the old days, so we were told, men were allowed inside its confines only to sleep and eat – or by invitation.*

men (first effected during the *wela*) – a bonding once vital for waging war, now necessary for the business of earning a living as migrant labourers in the city. At the same time it bonds the women as a powerful matriarchy, but without threatening the patriarchal role of the men. It is worth remembering that during the struggle against Kwa-Ndebele independence in the 1980s, it was the women as an organized and militant pressure group who played the leading role in preventing the South African and KwaNdebele plans from going ahead. Such is the power that is built into the Ndebele homestead.

## KWANDEBELE

The former homeland of KwaNdebele has a history of settlement that is at once triumphant and degraded, voluntary and forced, and it carries the signs of both on the face of its landscape. Driving out to the complex of villages around the Ndebele cultural and traditional centre at Weltevrede, one passes on either side of the road, scattered shack settlements seemingly dumped in the middle of nowhere. And that, in fact, is precisely how they came into being, the people living there having been rounded up in the urban areas where they were living before (mainly around Pretoria) and deposited there whether they wanted to live in the homeland or not. Invariably the sites lacked even the most basic amenities, and assistance from either the South African or the KwaNdebele government in establishing infrastructures was at best minimal.

It is a particularly sordid chapter in South African history that is written in these shack settlements, and even today, two decades later, their inhabitants are for the most part too busy with the business of survival to present us with much for our cultural delectation.

Deeper into KwaNdebele territory, however, the picture gradually changes, and even the forced removal sites at places like Wolwekraal have a different air about them. People here have found the resources to convert their sheet-iron shacks into more commodious and more settled dwellings, extending them, making gardens and fences around them, developing a type of homestead of shacks that is often as attractive as it is clearly livable.

Even here, however, is not what the consumer of Ndebele culture would like to consider the 'real Kwa-Ndebele'. That is a place which dates back to 1923, when the subjects of the Ndzundza royal heir Fene pooled resources to buy the farm Weltevrede, henceforth to be the centre of a reconstituted Ndzundza monarchy. By 1974, when the South African government bought up some 50 000 hectares of land on which to consolidate an

ABOVE: *An Ndebele homestead on a white-owned farm in the Middelburg district.*

ABOVE, RIGHT AND OPPOSITE: *With the establishment of the KwaNdebele homeland, some farms – particularly around Denilton and Verena – were sold by their white owners and taken over by those who had laboured on them; others were turned into free rural settlements. While the attitude of the people on such farms is generally welcoming, the differences in living conditions between the present and the past (under white ownership) are difficult to discern. The photographs on this and the following page were taken on one such farm, in the Verena district.*

PAGES 88-89: *The beasts represented on the walls of Maria Kabini's homestead in the village of Wolwekraal in KwaNdebele serve, according to her, as protectors. Though an uncharacteristic explanation for such motifs, the attribution of magical powers to homestead decoration fits with the quasi-magical functions associated with features like electric lights and telephone poles in Ndebele wall-decoration.*

PAGES 90-91: *Gates, doors and windows as observed in the villages of the former KwaNdebele homeland.*

Ndebele ethnic homeland, the area around Weltevrede had been settled by the Ndzundza for several decades. It is this region – in the proximity of the tribal authority structures whose centre was the royal kraal – that the most concerted expression of modern Ndebele material culture is to be found. It would nonetheless be a mistake to think that this is where the 'purest' expressions of Ndebele art and culture – for instance, the most representative homesteads – will be found. Quite the contrary, and there are good reasons why. One is that the farm Weltevrede was far from extensive. While what I have referred to as the Platonic Ndebele homestead is constructed on open land and can be developed in any direction more or less indefinitely, here land had to be parcelled out in standard-sized lots, each less than half the size of a playing field. The result was the creation of villages rather than traditional rural settlements and an enforced adaptation of lifestyle due to the change from the primarily cattle-based economy of the past. All the same, most households still possess a few head of cattle, though it is very unusual to find anything that could remotely be described as a herd.

Similarly, homestead design has had to accommodate changing circumstances. While the basic L- or U-shape continues to be the most characteristic form of ground-plan, the indefinite multiplication of living units within

the homestead is now curtailed by the boundary of the adjacent property, and thus such traditions as leaving undisturbed the ruins of the living quarters of the last generation have, in most instances, had to be abandoned. Likewise, the occupation of a single homestead site by an extended family is limited by the physical constraints of available space. Sons, therefore, on getting married, are as likely to apply for their own piece of land as they are to remain within the family homestead. It costs only around R10 per year to lease land from the king, and a visit to the royal kraal is all that is required. Thus, although the society has remained largely intact, its manifestations have changed considerably since the move to the former KwaNdebele homeland, and the homestead itself has become a curious hybrid of village and rural dwelling.

Such features as elaborately sculpted gateposts – elements of architecture that were primarily designed to create an impression from a distance, not from across the road – are nowadays relatively rare. Similarly, although the homestead is usually fronted by a walled courtyard, this is often itself contained within the perimeter of a chicken wire fence instead of the mud walls of earlier years.

In place of these former design elements – at least until the early 1980s – the women of KwaNdebele expressed their tribal pride and identity primarily through their

wallpainting, and it is in this region that the form reached its fullest (some would say most overblown) articulation. Certainly until the 1970s there were some villages where an unpainted home was a rarity. Today the overall picture is quite different. In many villages there is no decorative wallpainting whatsoever to be seen – except maybe in the occasional ruin bearing chipped and faded traces of a

former splendour. In others the occasional courtyard wall or window frame can be seen picked out in red or green floor polish or commercial paint – a passing salute to the past – among the uniform rows of Western-style bungalow housing that is gradually transforming the character of the former homeland.

## THE NEBO DISTRICT

In 1888, those members of the Ndzundza clan who were fortunate enough to be released from the forced servitude of their five-year indenture found themselves with hardly anywhere to go. For years the great mass of the people wandered through a wilderness of hostile farmers and merciless elements, seeking some simulacrum of the tribal structures that had once guaranteed their identity. Some of these traditionalists ended up at Hartebeestfontein, where Fene, heir to the Ndzundza throne, had been given work and where he was later joined by the old regent Nyabela. Some continued to wander for decades. A third group gravitated towards the vicinity of Kafferskraal (a mere 25 kilometres from the former seat of Ndzundza royal power), where Matsitsi, a half brother of Nyabela, had already established himself. According to Matsitsi, prior to the fall of the Ndzundza stronghold at Mapoch's Caves, he had been instructed by Nyabela to flee and establish a new Ndzundza authority and to rule in his (Nyabela's) place.

How true Matsitsi's claims actually were is hard to tell. Certainly, when Nyabela was released from prison in 1898, he did not attempt to join Matsitsi but Fene. Nevertheless, Matsitsi, once installed, had no intention of abdicating power, and hence yet another rift was forged in the ranks of the Ndebele – one that continues to this day.

The Matsitsi faction remained in the Kafferskraal area until the late 1930s, when, pressed for land by white settlement, the group was forced to move north, to the Nebo district. In 1956, the South African government acknowledged their right to the land by designating it the Nebo Trust Farms, to be administered according to broadly tribal principles by the heirs of Matsitsi. The fate of Nebo,

however, was more or less a foregone conclusion: it would be consolidated within one or other homeland, which it duly was (within the basically Sotho-Tswana-controlled homeland of Lebowa, which was formally constituted in the early 1970s).

It has been speculated that it is precisely because they have lived as a minority among other tribal groupings that the Nebo Ndzundza have clung more tenaciously to their customs through the 1980s and – thus far – the 1990s, than any other groups of Ndebele, even those closest to the Ndebele king in KwaNdebele itself. There is probably some truth in this: it was, after all, during their periods of greatest marginalization as a people that the Ndzundza of the royal faction flourished most notably as producers of culture. Once the threat of extinction had been removed with the establishment of the KwaNdebele homeland, custom began to lapse and, even more to the

*OPPOSITE AND BELOW: The Nebo district has remained more tradition-bound than other areas inhabited by the Ndebele. The black-and-white geometric designs, as seen on the walls of the homesteads opposite, are accorded the same magical properties as the old finger painting techniques. Sometimes though, as shown below, the use thereof is minimal.*

point, has been rapidly disappearing since the release of Nelson Mandela in 1990 and the concomitant promise of political freedom since the 1994 elections. Of course there are other factors that need to be taken into account, and on one level it makes hardly more sense to compare the histories of Nebo and KwaNdebele than it does to compare apples and pears, for although there is a common history, the authority structures to which the two groups have responded since the turn of the century have been very different.

Whatever the reasons, the pockets of Ndzundza still residing in the Nebo district seem to remain more conservative and to nurture their customs and traditional art forms with greater care than in any other territory inhabited by the Ndebele. In certain villages at least, there are (admittedly small) concentrations of women still wearing the traditional *dzilla* in profusion. Nowhere else, except in the special case of artists in areas frequented by tourists, is this the case. Equally striking is the fact that many women still possess and jealously guard their old-style traditional beadwork, some dating apparently from the early years of the century. What is more, they continue with the old tradition of handing such treasured beading down from mother to daughter through the generations. Though few allowed us to see these items, a number of women told us they continue to use old pieces in communing with the ancestors. Everywhere else fashion has overtaken tradition and the only beads the women still possess are those that the Nebo women scornfully dismiss as 'party-style' and completely unrecognizable to the ancestors.

If such characteristics suggest a greater degree of faith in the past, it is borne out in the wall decoration characteristically used by the women of Nebo. Strongly based in the old finger paintings of the nineteenth century, the definitively Nebo style in decorative wallpainting is purely geometric and executed solely in black and white on the retaining walls alone. Inside, in the layers of courtyard they often still build, there is seldom any decorative embellishment beyond coats of red and green floor polish – or occasionally, and entirely frivolously, painted slasto and imitation brickwork. As one woman explained, the visible Ndebeleness only needs to be at the entrance to the homestead to keep the evil spirits at bay. This, she insisted, was the real reason for painting on walls in the first place: it is for her, as it is for many of the Nebo women, an entirely magical, rather than a decorative, process.

Whether or not the motivation behind the wallpainting is earnest and magical, the effect is often splendid and pre-eminently visual. In the Nebo district, access to homesteads is still frequently through imposing sculpted

gateposts, and the architecture has more about it of the Platonic homestead design than we encountered anywhere else in Ndebele territory, except in isolated instances in the white-owned farmlands. In short, if one squints in villages with such improbable names as Vleisgevonden and Goedgedacht, it is often easy to imagine what a visual feast the heyday of Ndebele culture must have offered anyone visiting at the time.

Even today, something of the magic survives. In many ways the area feels as though, for all its rigours, it has been kept on 'hold'. For instance, we find at the top of a hill a woman by the name of Lettie Mahlangu. She tries to sell us beadwork which the representatives of Operation Hunger commissioned more than a year earlier but have

*OPPOSITE AND ABOVE: While the construction of such has all but died out elsewhere, gateposts in the Nebo district are often elaborate and sculptural items, complete with 'electric lights', 'postboxes' and 'gardens'.*

*PAGES 96-97: Many older women in the Nebo district continue to wear the metal dzilla – partly in fidelity to their husbands, partly in fidelity to tradition. Rose Skosana, featured on page 97 (left), is without dzilla because she is mourning the recent death of her husband, and custom demands that for a year thereafter she remove such adornments.*

PAGE 98: *The painted interior of Poppie Mahlangu's home at Goedgedacht in the Nebo district. She said she learnt the techniques of decorative wallpainting from a picture book.*
PAGE 99 AND BELOW: *The laying of a mud and dung floor in the traditional way. The surface is frequently renewed with layers of this plaster, and is often elaborately patterned.*

not collected. It is the standard party-style work. But then she produces an *ijogolo* (a married woman's apron) that she had completed only some months earlier. It has been made using 1960s-style beads – unpicked from a piece that had fallen apart. Its motifs, designs and proportions are convincingly of that era. She has worked in images of flatblocks with pillars at the corners, telephone poles, chimneys, the gamut of the domestic aspiration that lent such bitter-sweetness to the 1960s style. Only

one element places it in a new decade – the television aerial poking up behind the roof of the two-storey flat-block. On another hill we encounter Sophie Motha whose ancestors have told her that if she removes the dozens of *dzilla* she continues to wear around her legs, arms and neck, she will die. She tells us that she possesses a white beaded *mpoto* (a marriage apron) which she has left at the site where her familial ancestors lie buried, so it is not available for us to see. Meanwhile, as Sophie Motha walks stiff legged, and unnaturally straight backed, her children run around in Michael Jackson T-shirts, and a radio blares out cheap Motown.

In the village of Goedgedacht we find Poppie Mahlangu, a tiny woman, about 70 years old, who lives at the centre of a homestead which, being squeezed into a long and narrow space, has ended up as something like the Ndebele version of a row of semi-detached houses. Her house has elaborate gateposts but they are tatty and in much need of repair. She is a widow now, she says by way of apology, and has no will to keep up appearances. Her recent widowhood explains why she is not wearing *dzilla*. (For the period of a year, while she is in mourning, she has to remove them.)

Until some 20 years ago, Poppie Mahlangu tells us, she worked as a domestic in Johannesburg, but then she and her husband applied to the local chief for land – which was duly granted on the understanding that a sum of R10 be paid annually for its lease. She chuckles: 'But we don't pay that any more. There was a boycott. The chief was supposed to be building roads and getting us water, but he wasn't doing anything, so we stopped paying him.'

If Poppie Mahlangu has ceased 'giving unto Caesar', she has not ceased giving to the gods. She tells us she is a Christian, but she sleeps every night with her Middelburg blanket, because her understanding is that the ancestors will punish her if she fails to do so. The blanket in question has only two beaded strips worked on its surface; this also is in pursuance of a specific instruction from the ancestors. She says they told her that it would lead to harm if she were to have more, but she has no explanation of why – even though the ancestors regularly appear to her while she is sleeping.

'How do they appear?' I ask. I am wondering if she will explain the visits in terms of dreams or in more literal ways, but she understands the question in a different light.

'They used to wear beads when I was younger,' she says, 'but now they follow the people, and come in ordinary clothes.' It is an interesting thought, though not picked up by any other informant: the ancestors themselves in the process of changing. We are sitting inside Poppie

Mahlangu's painted interior when she tells me this. It is a darkly atmospheric place with some fairly standard painting on the walls: houses, electric lights, and so on – the inspiration for which, she tells me, she found not in the cities during her years as a domestic worker but in a book on Ndebele art. Along the walls are built-in ledges and storage spaces, such as only the older houses have these days, but even here they are mixed in with melamine tables and chairs and a calendar (some years old) advertising a garage somewhere. It is a melancholy mix of the old and the new.

She is terribly afraid, Poppie tells me. Her daughter has lost her traditional values and she is afraid the daughter will not bury her according to custom when she dies: she will get cold in her grave until the proper rites are performed, and she will not be taken into the ranks of the ancestors. It is the fear of the traditional Ndebele as the new world swallows up the old.

## FARMLANDS

When the Boers won the war against the Ndzundza Ndebele in 1883, their revenge against the troublesome followers of Nyabela was swift and devastating. With their leaders executed or imprisoned and their lands confiscated, the people were placed under a five-year period of indenture as labourers, with first claim to their services being given to burghers who had served in the commando that had defeated them. Now, as historian Peter Delius records in his essay 'The Ndzundza Ndebele: Indenture and the Making of Ethnic Identity, 1883-1914', the Boer commando in question was drawn mainly from the following districts: Lydenburg, Middelburg, Standerton, Wakkerstroom, Potchefstroom and Pretoria. It was thus to these areas that the Ndzundza were dispersed, and although in places like Standerton and Potchefstroom the Ndzundza have tended to lose their specific tribal identity, it is in these areas that the Southern Ndebele continue to be found on white-owned farms.

The terms of the indenture, as has already been noted in chapter one, were peculiarly harsh, and amounted to little less than outright enslavement – though, with sour irony, they were presented in ZAR edicts as constituting a 'humanitarian' gesture. In theory, farm owners were required to pay a sum not exceeding £3 to each family per year, but in fact very few of the Ndzundza received anything like that meagre sum, since payments in kind, such as food and clothing, were included. Furthermore, the annual wage of £3 was to be offset against a war fine of £5, payable by the farmer on behalf of each Ndzundza family.

The one and only concession granted to the Ndzundza was that they were given patches of land on which to grow crops for their subsistence and, if they had any, to keep their straggling cattle.

This is the grim background to Ndzundza life on today's white-owned farmlands, and it is worth repeating because, in some places at least, hardly anything has changed over the intervening century. In many cases the farmers simply refused to release their pools of essentially free labour at the conclusion of the period of indenture – nor were they forced by the state to do so. In other cases, having nowhere else to go, the labourers chose to stay.

ABOVE: *Particularly in areas where paints are hard to come by, dramatic effects are obtained by the simplest of means. In this homestead on a white-owned farm in the Middelburg area, the brown mud of the walls has merely been framed with bands of whitewash.*

Now, a hundred years later, in the Stofberg district, we drive past a row of posters advertising meetings of white right-wing organizations, before turning to negotiate a bumpy track that leads to what looks like a decorated homestead set on a low hill. Painted mainly with washing blue and with doors and windows picked out in a powder made from the oxidized residues of batteries, it does indeed turn out to be an Ndebele dwelling. There is little that is remarkable about it, though. It is just a very basic U-shape structure, poorly thatched and decorated in the most rudimentary of ways. The homestead is fronted by a low wall the entrance of which is framed with gateposts, but both wall and posts are under repair and are wrapped in plastic at this moment. The sitting ledges built into the outside face of the wall are uncovered though, and it is here that we sit talking to Jaseph Mahlangu.

Although he looks easily old enough to have personally fought in Mapoch's Wars, Jaseph Mahlangu says it was in fact his father who had been one of Nyabela's warriors and subject to the indenture. Jaseph himself was born only around 1900, on the farm Swartkoppies, and it is there, looking out over the lands that make up that farm, that we find him today. Jaseph tells us that although he worked as a labourer from before his teens until well into his seventies, he has never received a day's wage in his life, but he

has been allowed to keep between six and eight cows, and to work a small patch of land to grow food. This has been enough to keep him here, though even in his old age it does not come free. When we arrive, there is one member of the homestead who is absent – Jaseph's grandson Timothy. He is out working in the white farmer's fields and, so Jaseph tells us, he also receives no wage. Because Jaseph is still living there, Timothy must work for free. If Jaseph did not have a grandson to work on his behalf, he would be turned off the land to fend for himself. It has happened to a number of his contemporaries, he says.

In fairness, Jaseph's case is extreme. Most of the white farmers nowadays do pay some kind of wage to the descendants of the indentured Ndzundza. In some cases it is a specified number of bags of mealie meal; in others it is a cash wage which varies from R30-R300 per month. And though many of the Ndzundza continue to fear eviction once they are no longer able to provide the farmer with labour, in other cases there is more humanity at work.

Driving along the main road between Middelburg and Belfast, near the Middelburg Dam, many travellers see, but do not remark on, an Ndebele-painted homestead set half a kilometre back from the road. It belongs to Betty Mahlangu, and it is on the farm Rondebosch. Betty heads a large and complex household with, as far as could be

BELOW AND OPPOSITE BELOW: *Rustic aesthetics: decorated gates and doors from Ndebele homesteads on white-owned farms. Note the use of earth pigments, washing blue, charcoal and whitewash, and the way that junk is recycled to often dramatic effect.*

ascertained, four sons and about a dozen women and assorted children. None of them actually works for the owner of the farm; the sons are either at school or at work in nearby Middelburg, and the labour of the women is not needed. Nevertheless, the farmer has allowed them to stay on after the death of Betty's husband.

Betty, in large measure attributes this to the good offices of the ancestors and to her continued observance of Ndebele custom. 'Wallpainting does not come from the ancestors,' she confides, 'but they like it. If the walls were not painted, Uys [the farmer] would chase us away.'

In this spirit of traditional self-interest, Betty Mahlangu continues to wear the *dzilla* and to shave her head in the old traditional manner. She also has, tattooed into her skin, a line that runs down the centre of the forehead to the tip of the nose. It is a tribal marking and is to be found in a number of photographs taken of Ndebele women in the early decades of the century, but Betty Mahlangu was the only woman we saw thus marked today. She had no explanation of the marking beyond that it was traditional.

Betty Mahlangu's homestead is an extensive, rambling affair – it has to be to accommodate the many women and children who emerged from the various dwellings on our arrival – but it still follows the basic U-plan of the Ndebele living complex. A central rectangular structure is flanked on either side by smaller dwellings, and set back and to the sides there are constructions used as service rooms – a kitchen, a laundry, a nursery, and so on.

The outer wall of the forecourt to the homestead is adorned with a chevron design in ochre and with black and white lines painted on a turquoise ground. Despite the proximity of Middelburg – it lies barely 10 kilometres down the road – Betty Mahlangu has used ground earth pigment for the ochre, and old battery oxide or charcoal to make black. These are the techniques, she tells us, that she learnt from her mother when she was barely more than a child at the farm Lemoenfontein, some kilometres to the north, and in fact she still goes to Lemoenfontein to fetch the raw materials from which the ochre is made.

In the courtyard the homestead decoration is sparser, with only the façade of the central structure favoured with the chevrons, though this time in blues and greens in place of the ochre on the outer wall. For the rest of the buildings, only the odd wall is painted (in the same turquoise as is used on the outer wall), and the odd doorway and window are outlined with black and white.

Whereas the outside of Betty Mahlangu's homestead is identifiably, and even typically, Ndebele, inside it is the usual mixture of the traditional and the acculturative. Inside the cooking hut there is a sight that we have seen in

ABOVE AND OPPOSITE: *Contrasting and harmonizing colours work together in planar formations to create an almost painterly sense of space.*

any number of other Ndebele dwellings: the coal stove in the corner, polished to immaculacy, and some feet away the depression in the dung flooring, with charred bits of stick and the pot resting on its three legs, still holding the remains of the last family meal. In the main living space there is the ubiquitous, out-of-date calendar; there are portraits of leaders of the Christian Zion Church in frames; and hanging alongside these the 'pomet', which establishes Betty Mahlangu as a woman of traditional standing in the district. But it is in the rooms of the sons of the household that the real pathos of cultural crossovers is manifest, etched on the walls in the form of girlie

pictures from local soft porn magazines. All of the models posing provocatively and availably on the walls are white. Some have been annotated, one with the addition of a needle and thread in reference to the Afrikaans word *naai*, which is slang for copulation but politely means 'to sew'. Another bears the legend in Afrikaans: 'You can marry him – but watch out.' Yet another has painted alongside it on the wall, in dashes of red paint, a clumsy heart shape – somehow the most helpless gesture of all.

A different time, a different road. We visit dozens of the Ndebele settlements that are dotted around the Eastern Transvaal landscape, usually at the bitter end of tortuous tracks. We find that particularly in the Roossenekal area (the traditional seat of the Ndzundza) the phlegmatic welcome we are accustomed to receiving is seldom forthcoming. We are treated with reserve, shyness and, not infrequently, something that is not far from outright hostility. Numerous informants meet our questions with the rebuff that this is 'our culture' – in other words, it is not available for outside prying. We also notice that the dogs, which are to be found at every homestead, do not wag their tails on our approach, and on more than one occasion photographer Mark Lewis has to scamper away from a promising composition to protect the seat of his pants. Later, in the same area, driving through acres of mealie fields, we are all but pushed off the road by a white farmer dressed in khakis and sporting on his windshield the insignia of the neo-Nazi Afrikaner Weerstandsbeweging.

Sometimes the Ndebele settlements on the farms are of the order of whole villages. One such is on the farm Ongesiens, between Middelburg and Stoffberg, where

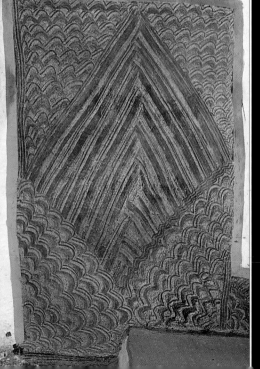

around 300 people live in a cluster that boasts its own farm school, which is jointly sponsored by the old black education authority, the Department of Education and Training, and the farmer. Here life is relatively comfortable and the people are friendly. They invite us to attend a female initiation celebration on the weekend, but we catch them unawares nevertheless and nobody – except the girls who have undergone the initiation and are on display – has dressed traditionally for the occasion.

Other settlements are much smaller clusters of houses; yet others comprise only a single homestead. Though many still have traces of geometric wallpainting, only on a handful has the painting been renewed. Far more common is the much older style of decoration in which earth pigments of local origin – or store-bought oxides – are used in broad, flat planes with only the borders picked out for contrast. Many of these homesteads are remarkably beautiful and idyllic in appearance, either blending in their earth colours with the dominant coloration of the landscape, or picking up the colours of the sky in dazzling blues edged with white.

One homestead in particular stands out. It is located close to the main road from Middelburg, just short of the turn-off to Belfast. It has been built in such a way as to create a central courtyard, without a painted façade, and is completely enclosed by ramshackle buildings. Here the decoration is all inward facing – that is, into the central courtyard and the minor courtyards created by low walls. While the occasional wall has been picked out in ochres and blues, the dominant decorative effect is provided by the old-style finger painting technique executed with a pale yellowish sand.

To the visitor this is a fairy tale environment, with tiny goats rubbing their muzzles against our legs and climbing over the furniture indoors, and naked children disporting themselves in the nooks of the courtyard. But Hezekiel Sithole, the youth I am talking to, has little interest in his idyll. He has an oily soft perm in his hair, and when he learns that I work as a journalist, he wants to know about the ANC's land policies. Will the Ndebele be getting their land back after all this time in the wilderness? I do not have the heart to tell him the truth: that in terms of agreements struck in multi-party negotiations in 1992 and 1993, and in terms of the ANC's Reconstruction and Development Programme, the answer is 'No'. The land was seized before the 1913 Land Act, which has been taken to mark the start of the period in which reparations may be negotiated. Whatever happened before 1913 is taken as old history, which can no longer be undone.

'I'm not sure,' I tell Hezekiel. 'It's very complicated.'

*OPPOSITE, LEFT AND BELOW: The homestead featured in this series of pictures is the one located between Belfast and Middelburg where we met Hezekiel Sithole.*

CHAPTER 5

# BEADS AND ADORNMENTS

*Though in some circumstances beadwork is also worn by men, it belongs primarily to the women of the Ndebele. Through the varieties of beadwork, the entire life of the woman is mapped out, from birth to distinguished matronhood. But, more and more, as the appetite of collectors grows, the original purposes are being lost.*

ABOVE: *'Every bead you see in indigenous southern African art represents a transaction between whites and blacks.' Rayda Becker, director of the Gertrude Posel Gallery, University of the Witwatersrand.*

OPPOSITE: *An Ndebele woman wearing the beaded marriage blanket or* nguba. *Some women told us they add a strip of beading to the blanket with each passing year of marriage, resulting in such elaborate items as that shown here.*

Regrettably, we do not know nearly as much as we would like to about the origins of bead-working in sub-Saharan Africa, nor about how and why beads came to play such a central part in the material culture of the South Nguni tribes.

As far as the Ndebele are concerned, the demonstrable history of beadworking goes back only as far as the second half of the nineteenth century, when Europeans bearing beads of Czechoslovakian origin penetrated the hinterland and came into contact with the people living in the present-day Eastern Transvaal. It would be naïve, though, to think that this represents the first time the Ndebele had been exposed to beads in any form. Nor, one might venture, is it enough to merely refer in vague terms to possible practices of stringing seed pods and suchlike together and assume that out of this grew the splendour of Ndebele beadwork – as many writers on the subject have done.

The plain fact is that the actual beadwork produced by Ndebele women in the later nineteenth century is of such a quality and degree of elaboration that it would suggest a long and developed tradition. Besides, we have evidence of a widespread trade in manufactured beads within the southern African subcontinent that predates by several centuries the first known Ndebele pieces.

When the Portuguese landed on the east coast of Africa in 1495 and made contact with the indigenes near present-day Maputo on the coast of Mozambique, they were far from being the first foreign traders in the area. Busy exchanges had already been pursued between the people of southern Africa and those from the East for upwards of three centuries, and possibly a lot longer. Recent archaeological work has discovered in the sub-continent, beads of Indian origin dating from the eleventh and twelfth centuries. Porcelain beads, as well as evidences of trade with the East, have also been unearthed in some of the numerous stone 'Zimbabwes', or royal courts, located in the country which today takes its name from them.

The empire of Monomatopa – which archaeologists agree was that of a Shona civilization, arising out of the great Bantu migrations of the first few centuries AD – was not only a powerful military presence, dominating the subcontinent, but also a trading culture. In fact, evidence suggests that it reached its pre-eminence in southern and central Africa precisely by trading with the East, exchanging in particular gold and raw materials gleaned from the area of its influence for manufactured goods.

Although this is more conjecture than fact, it is nevertheless probable that the Shona of Zimbabwe would have had contact with their cousins, the South Nguni, who for several centuries had been established in the areas that lay between the seat of the empire and the Zimbabwean ports of trade on the Mozambique coast. While this is taking something of a leap of faith, there may well have been a connection between the Shona traders, or at least their Eastern suppliers, and some earlier traditions of beadworking among the Nguni.

Without a strong theory line such as those suggested above, it becomes difficult to account for the ubiquity of beadworking traditions within the South Nguni language group as a whole. We know that the South Nguni had fragmented into subgroupings long before the arrival of the Europeans, yet beads perform remarkably similar functions in the various tribal groupings despite their having been distinct from one another for half a millennium or more. The Ndebele, the clans we refer to collectively as Zulus, and those we know as Xhosas all share a highly articulated 'language' of beadwork in which beads are used to reflect the lives and status of girls and women. In each of these cases, as in others among the South Nguni, beads serve to define, to mark out the stages of and, in anthropological terminology, to regulate the lives of females in the society. More simply, certain items of beadwork, worn particularly in ceremonial contexts, will indicate the age of the wearer, whether she has undergone ritual initiation, whether she is married or single, whether she has produced children, and so on. Now, to say the least of it, it is difficult to accept that such highly formalized usages could have evolved independently of one another. And if the similarities are not coincidental, then some root tradition must have been in place many centuries ago – long before the penetration of the hinterland by the nineteenth-century Dutch trekkers and English colonists.

Certainly, common sense tells us that Ndebele beadwork of the mid-nineteenth century – the earliest known examples – do not represent a new or emerging tradition. And common sense is most insistent on this point: that the objects are not what a person would spontaneously create when presented with a bag of beads for the first time. Nor are they regarded as such in the view of the Ndebele themselves.

The evidence of the oral historian is that beadworking constitutes an ancient tradition which has been passed down for more generations than anyone can remember, but as far as could be determined during the course of our fieldwork, there is no memory, however mythologized, of when beadworking actually began. Even the oldest women we spoke to – and some were well over ninety years of age – talked about their mothers and grandmothers telling them that they in turn had been instructed by their mother and grandmothers.

But while we might postulate the existence of ancient traditions, such supposition, it should be noted, raises as many questions as it suggests answers. If there were indeed older beads, why have none come down to us? Why are the earliest existing pieces composed entirely of

ABOVE: *Ancestors sometimes prescribe in dreams just how much beading a marriage blanket should carry. It is not unusual to find some belonging to elderly women yet bearing only a single strip of beadwork.*

The possibility of Zimbabwean mediation, however, is merely one speculative scenario – there are others that are equally plausible. Trade between north and south-central Africa may have long predated the Monomatopan civilization, and the north of Africa had for centuries before the birth of Christ been in contact with not only Europe but also the civilizations of Asia. The answers, in the final analysis, lie in archaeology; but archaeology has, at the risk of a poor pun, barely begun to scratch the surface of the African continent.

TOP: *Unmarried girls at a female initiation ceremony. The stiff beaded apron they wear is known as an* isiphephetu. *It is worn by unmarried girls who have already undergone their period of seclusion. According to one source the isiphephetu is traditionally stiff and unwieldy in order, at least symbolically, to enforce chastity. Married women's aprons have more flexible materials as a base.*

LEFT, ABOVE AND PAGE 112: *As is the case with mural art, Ndebele beadwork is made exclusively by the women. Beads from older pieces are often recycled to make various beaded items thought to be more in line with modern fashions.*

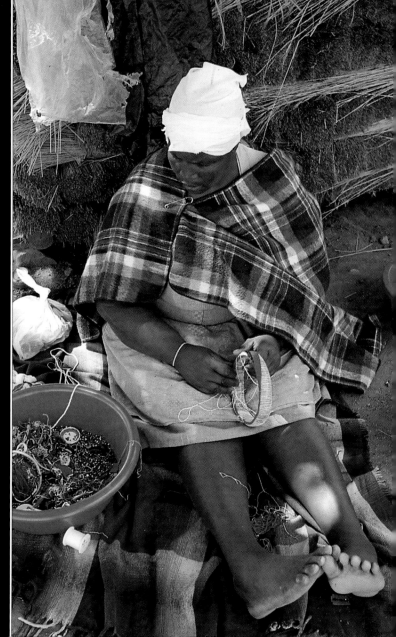

nineteenth-century Czechoslovakian beads? What happened to the older pieces? Why were the old beads not incorporated, as is the custom today, into pieces made from the newly available European ones? Had the customs centred around beadworking gone into abeyance, to be revived when the beads became available again?

Or is it the case that tradition itself changed at some point? Two older informants did suggest that this might indeed be so. What they said was that in the ancient tribal custom, beadwork was buried along with its owner as apparel to be worn in the deceased's new incarnation as an ancestor. But at some point, and for reasons unknown, this tradition changed, according to these informants, and it became traditional for a woman to pass down at least some of her beadwork to her daughter or another relative from the next generation.

## CLASSIC WHITE BEADWORK

It is not until the latter years of the nineteenth century that we can do anything more than speculate around the subject of Ndebele beadwork. Here we find, dating from the 1880s, about the time of the defeat of the Ndzundza at Mapoch's Caves, the earliest pieces of Ndebele beadwork that have come down to us.

By the time these were produced the Ndebele were already well established in the Eastern Transvaal. Through trade with Europeans they were able to obtain the delicate, small beads that are characteristic of the old-style beadwork. Distinctively, these old pieces are overwhelmingly made from closely worked white beads, merely punctuated by sparse geometric designs picked out in colour.

It is not merely the rarity and age of such pieces that make them probably the most prized of all the artefacts of the Ndebele. There is also a distinctive care and a craftsmanship in their manufacture that is difficult to find at any other point in the known history of Ndebele beadwork; though as one informant cited by my co-worker, Mark Hurwitz, said, when a woman had made up the full range of her traditional beadwork – aprons, marriage veil, cape, beaded blanket, and so on – 'she never saw very well again'.

The patient skill required for such detail, deployed as it was with relatively irregular beads – although manufactured, not standardized the way they tend to be today – makes for eminently collectable objects of exquisite and manifest quality.

At the same time the simplicity of the designs – usually the most minimal of geometric and linear motifs

picked out against the textures of the white beading – is particularly sympathetic to a Western sensibility steeped in notions of classic harmony and symmetry.

## CHANGING STYLES IN A CHANGING WORLD

As was the case in the so-called classical styles in Western art, simpler harmonies gradually gave way to innovation, and the inevitable processes of stylistic evolution came into play. By the 1920s and the 1930s new subject matter has crept in. White beads are no longer as dominant as they have been; coloured beads, particularly oranges, greens, blues and reds, begin to play a more important part in the overall composition.

In part, the shift can be attributed to the availability of new ranges of beads in the trading stores and, one might conjecture, to the unavailability of the old Czechoslovakian beads, but at the same time there is a significant evolution in design, with motifs becoming increasingly representational as time goes by.

It is important to put the question of motifs into context. Although many writers on the subject have missed this point, Ndebele women confirm that even in certain very old pieces of beadwork – that is, those dating from around the turn of the century – at least some of the basic symbolism is associated with the domestic environment. Of course, the symbolism is radically abstracted; what is being represented is more like an idea of a homestead than the appearance of a homestead. While the relationships are not readily legible between the domestic environment and the actual designs, the principle is made more accessible if one thinks in terms of the bird's-eye viewpoint. Thus a common motif, such as the 'transformative H' – often with a double bar and equally often with 'feet' growing off the extremities – becomes associated with the groundplan of an Ndebele homestead. It is a kind of enclosure – at least quasi-magically evoked.

This line of interpretation, however, should not be taken too far. While various informants, particularly the older women, did explain the root symbolism in terms such as these, symbolism in the old beadwork is not primarily visual but hieratic, caught up with religious belief and traditions of the sacredness of spaces. Therefore it cannot be read simply by looking at it, and the task is not made any easier by discussing the question with the Ndebele women themselves. The women still use symbols like the transformative H, the rows of axe-heads and the so-called 'spanner', particularly in wallpainting,

ABOVE: *Nowadays the more complex pieces of beadwork are most often made for sale rather than for ceremonial use. Generally the quality of such pieces is desperately inferior, but a few beadworkers, like Martha Mahlangu who lives at Bundu Inn, have risen to the challenge, making work in the new styles without sacrificing the standards of the old.*

PAGES 114-115: *Examples of the oldest Ndebele beadwork that has come down to us. These pieces date from around 1880 to around 1920. It is one of the mysteries of research into the Ndebele that no older pieces have come to light, though one possible explanation is that before Mapoch's War, a woman's beadwork was buried along with her.*

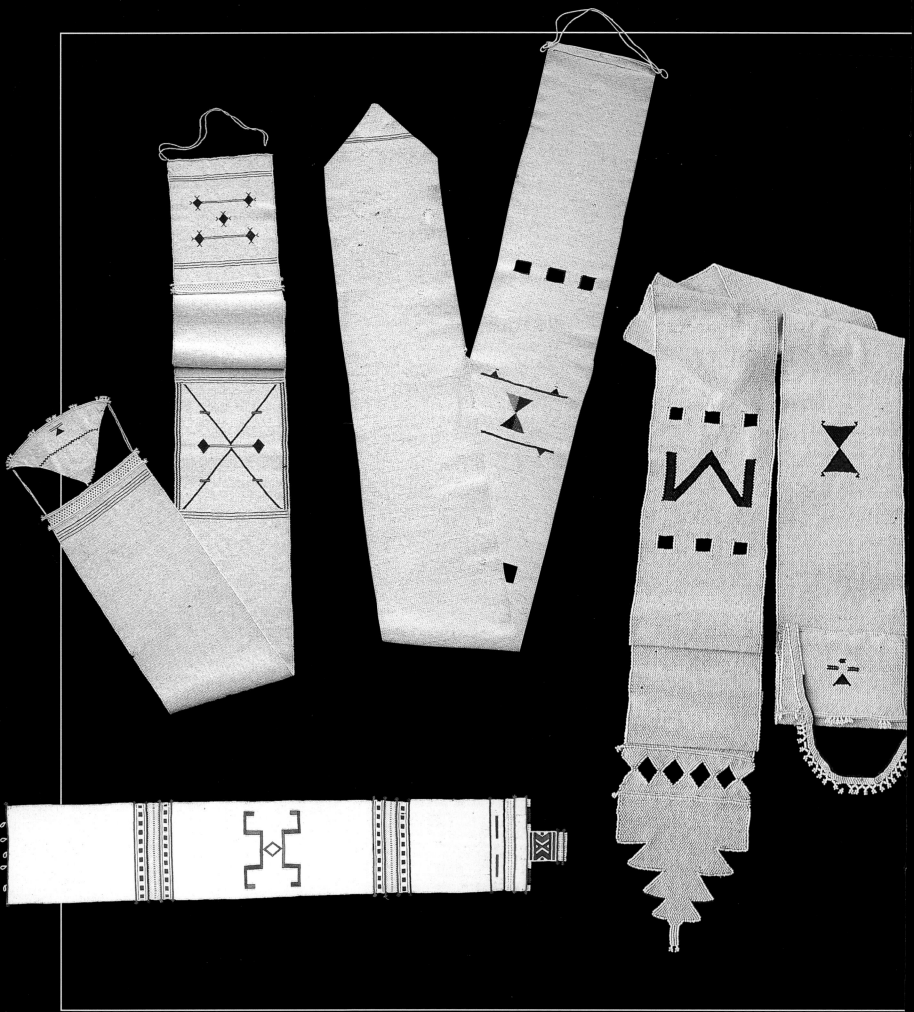

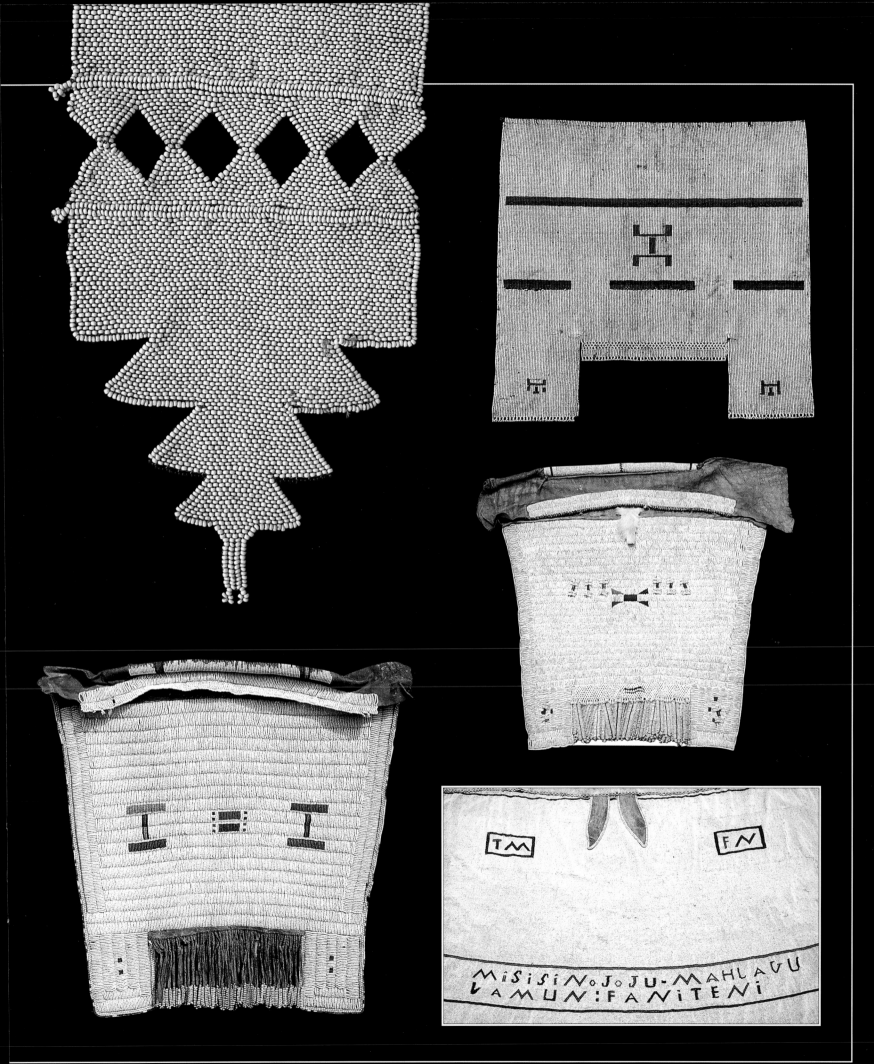

MiSiSiN₀J₀JU-MAHLAGU
VAMUN:FANiTENi

More important here, however, is how the tradition changes. Gradually, from the 1920s and 1930s onwards, the representation of the domestic environment becomes increasingly more literal, and houses and other domestic appurtenances are 'drawn' in the beadwork. For the most part in this period, abstract motifs tend to be relegated to a secondary role, the major focus being placed on stylized representations of thatched huts, singly or in groups. The huts are now seen as though from ground level. According to older informants the distinction between single and multiple representations of huts follows distinctions in wealth or social status, but many, particularly the younger women differ in this view, suggesting instead that the number of huts represented is more a design decision than one rooted in quantitive symbolism. It is possible that both are right: what used to be a relatively rigid and hieratic usage has lapsed into something more decoratively charged.

Decoration, though, is not the only issue here. Notably from the 1940s onwards, women's beadwork increasingly carries a record of aspiration rather than documentary truth. Around this time new sets of motifs start creeping in — many as contemporary interpretations of traditional symbols. One of these is yet another variation on the H-shape discussed above; now, placed at the head of a vertical bar of beading, it comes to represent a telephone pole. The old triangles of 'axe-heads' now come to represent electric lights, while the form of the hut itself undergoes a transformation. In the pieces from the 1920s and 1930s it is represented by a pair of opposing zigzags topped with an overhanging shape like a triangle with the top lopped off. In the 1940s it is represented by the classic hut formula — a rectangle with a triangle on top. According to informants, the change corresponds to that from the grass hut — depicted according to traditional formula — to the mud and dung constructions that the Ndebele have built since the time of the Ndzundza king, Mabhogo.

'I learnt from my mother how to make the old grass houses in my beads,' Betty Ntuli, from the KwaNdebele village of Waterval B, explained. 'But then I changed that. I wanted to keep up with the times, and nowadays houses are not made like that, so I put the new roof on, and I put in chimneys. The houses we live in have chimneys but the old beadwork didn't know how to put in the chimneys.'

This is just the beginning of the transformation. In much of the beadwork the huts give way to what the Ndebele women typically refer to as 'flats', introducing vertically layered 'windows' to suggest different storeys.

ABOVE, RIGHT AND OPPOSITE: *Between the early years of this century and the 1930s and 1940s, Ndebele beadworking underwent significant changes, with the overall — and only minimally punctuated — white of the older pieces gradually giving way to geometric shapes and to the beginnings of domestic imagery. This development is illustrated in this sequence of examples.*

but, by their own account, they use them merely as domestic charms. The belief system in which such things were immediately meaningful has long since passed. Only the observance remains, and one is left in a situation akin to trying to make sense of a crucifix without the Bible.

Often something close to a whole skyline is essayed, with complexes of roofs matched up with electric lights, telephone poles, etc. In the same stylistic development, patches of green are often introduced at the base of the represented buildings and these are usually described as gardens; vertical bars refer to fence posts, and so on.

What this amounts to is a shift in function of some significance – a gear change from hieratic to more secular kinds of representation. Though the artists of the Ndebele continue to use many of the same devices, the meanings and significances of these change completely as the women assimilate and digest through their beadwork a new world, dominated as it is by the values and the technologies of the West. Nowhere is the process spelt out with more poignancy than in the motif of the zigzag wall. Gradually freed from the hut shape it comes to represent a flight of stairs leading up to the modern housing that is represented.

It is perhaps pertinent to note at this point that, even today, the vast majority of areas occupied by the Ndebele do not have electricity, nor multistorey buildings. The modernity that is being essayed in the beadwork of the later periods has more to do with wish than it does with fact. Many women explained the choice of motifs in the beadwork explicitly in these terms, saying that the represented image was how they wanted their houses to look, and that all the paraphernalia – the electric lights, the telephone poles, the chimneys, and so on – represented the things they wanted to possess.

In a sense, then, there is a process of symbolic appropriation at work. The world of the white suburbs, in real life seen only from the vantage of the domestic servant, is at some level being owned, or wished, in and through the domestic imagery of the beadwork. But while this is undeniably true, not too much should be made of it. There is not a great deal of seriousness attached to the symbolism of the beadwork, and while the significances may once have been profound, nowadays one feels there is more of a spirit of formal and often fanciful inventiveness at play than a ritual seriousness at work.

## NDEBELE POP STYLES OF THE 1960s

The look of Ndebele beadwork produced during the 1960s is markedly different from that of the 1940s and 1950s. The white background becomes something of a rarity and is supplanted by much more insistent deep greens, blues and black. The beads themselves are slightly bigger (and, happily for the women beadworkers, equipped with larger eyes).

In general, architectural motifs become far bolder. Flatblocks, electric lights and the other hallmarks of modernity become more dominant and common as motifs, a shift which has led many authors to infer that developments in Ndebele wallpainting provided the major impetus for the change. Perhaps the most striking difference, though, is that produced by the use of deep

PAGES 118-119: *Examples of the 1960s style in Ndebele beadworking. This commonly given category is often deceptive, since the so-called 1960s style dominated production until the 1980s. In fact, the piece featured on page 119 at bottom left was made in the 1990s out of beads taken from an older piece.*

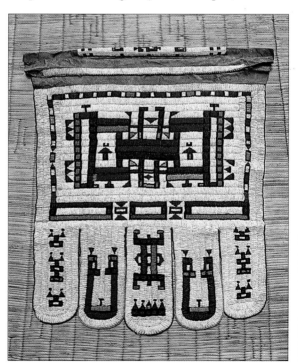

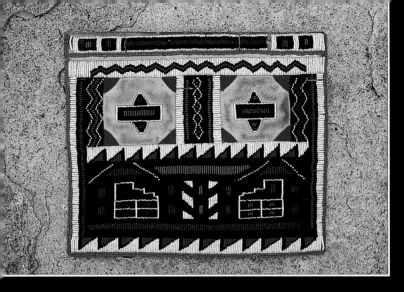

greens and blues as background, the immediate effect being an overall geometric design rather than one of motifs picked out against a neutral ground.

In large measure these changes would appear, again, to be attributable to the availability of new ranges of beads in the trading stores of the Eastern Transvaal – in particular, beads of French manufacture with less translucence and favouring the deeper blues, greens and purples, and making black available for the first time. Using these beads led, in most cases, to a jazzier, funkier product with a minimal use of white – this mainly appearing as an accent or for contrast.

Nevertheless, this does not tell the whole story. One of the most important, though least immediately definable, of the factors determining stylistic change in Ndebele beadwork has been the growth of a tourist market. The emergence of the 1960s style of beadwork seems closely to have accompanied the creation in the 1950s of KwaMsiza, north of Pretoria. It is here, as far as can be ascertained, that the new style made its first appearance.

Although the majority of the beadwork being produced by the Ndebele was not specifically being made for sale, it is around this time that the first collectors of Ndebele beadwork started to move about the rural areas. The injections of much-needed cash were welcomed in households impoverished by dispossession and the inexorable depression suffered as a result of the government's apartheid policies. The thought of selling pieces of beadwork – even family heirlooms – that could be remade at a later stage was therefore no longer anathema.

Significantly enough, it is also around this time that the beadwork begins, noticeably, to diversify. Whereas in the past beadworking had been largely confined to the traditional forms – aprons, wedding regalia, the ritualized expressions of tribal life-cycles – now a more decorative impulse becomes clearly discernible in the craft. Mugs are beaded, incidental necklaces and bracelets begin to be made, the fertility dolls, which in the old system were made only on the occasion of marriage, are now produced in profusion and mainly for sale. Such items as *golwani*, traditionally beaded in monochrome, are now frequently treated as canvases on which to develop characteristically 'Ndebele' motifs. At the same time new motifs make their appearance, some merely decorative, others like the so-called 'Ufly', or aeroplane, reflecting in immediate ways the assimilation of Western technologies and values.

Despite the new look of the 1960s' beadwork, the differences between it and the beadwork made in the 1940s and 1950s are more apparent than real. The 1960s style

merely takes a step further the response to a hegemonic Western culture that is already present in the earlier work, developing in the process its own languages, its own forms, its own possibilities and inventions. For the observer it has its own fascination, especially in the ways in which it adapts to and registers the forces shaping the late colonial society. It is in this light that one should look at a development in traditional usage that comes to the fore during the 1960s – the emergence of the so-called '*plastici*', the apron in which plastic strips and cut-outs came to replace the blocks and strips of coloured beading.

While many commentators have been inclined to dismiss the plastic as an aberration or abomination within the beadworking tradition, the Ndebele would not necessarily agree with them. *Plastici* are worn at tribal ceremonies and festivities, and as far as the Ndebele themselves are concerned, there is no difference between their traditional value and status and those of their more painstakingly beaded counterparts.

There is some irony, however, in the fact that *plastici* are made less and less in contemporary Ndebele society. Though powerfully emerging during the 1960s and the 1970s, the making of the kinds of plastic aprons that could be considered as art has lapsed significantly in recent times. The reason, so several informants told us, is largely attributable to the fact that the tourist market has only the most minimal interest in anything other than beaded items. Thus plastics have latterly been relegated to the most minor of roles within the structures of Ndebele material culture; only the occasional back skirt, or *isithimba*, may be seen, its desultory design picked out in masking tape or insulation tape and not much more that. Appropriately enough in this changing world, such items are made essentially as one-offs, to be worn at a particular ceremony then cast aside. Disposable tradition.

## CONTEMPORARY BEADING PARTY STYLE

If the relationship between the makers of Ndebele beadwork and its market has complicated its production since the 1960s, it was during the 1980s that the market came to assume a thoroughly determinate role.

What is particularly at issue here is the role of Operation Hunger, a nationwide self-help scheme which, during the early 1980s, identified the potential of Ndebele beadworking as a way of generating some kind of economy within the depressed areas occupied by

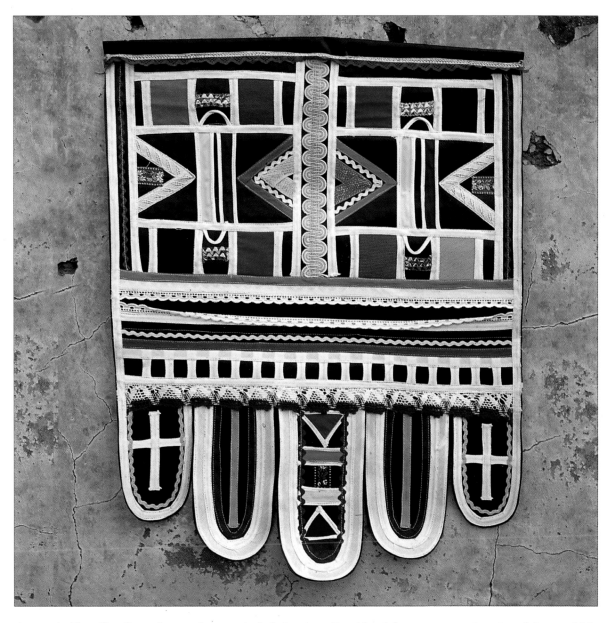

OPPOSITE AND LEFT: *During the 1960s a new trend developed among the Ndebele of making traditional 'beaded aprons' out of plastic strips, bias binding and various other surprisingly disposable materials. The fashion did not last more than a decade, but some pieces of remarkable interest, both visually and culturally have come down to us.*

PAGES 122-125: *The original Ndebele doll was hooped and Michelin Man-like – as depicted by those on page 122. Such dolls were usually presented to young nubile girls as fertility charms, although similar dolls are often used by sangomas as well. As time went on (from around the 1970s onwards), however, commercial forces and cross-cultural aesthetic influences came into play, and Ndebele dolls began to undergo significant transformations. The dolls became increasingly representational and decreasingly symbolic. Today it is not uncommon to find Western-style dolls transformed with Ndebele beadworking – these particular forms ending the sequence.*

the people. Travelling from place to place, particularly in KwaNdebele and the Nebo district, its representatives made beads available to the women, placed orders for saleable items, then returned on the next round trip to collect the finished products for sale via the organization's local and international outlets.

One of the effects of the relatively centralized beadworking industry to which Operation Hunger has given rise is that beadworking is becoming an increasingly specialized pursuit among the Ndebele. It is no longer the case that all girls will be taught the techniques around the time of initiation. Nor is it uncommon for young women or their mothers to commission other women to produce ritual beadwork on their behalf. The next step is to buy it, so to speak, off the shelf.

Considered from an economic point of view – which is the only one that really concerns a philanthropic body like Operation Hunger – the project has proved more than a moderate success, having largely achieved its stated aim of generating money in seriously impoverished rural areas. This remains true even though in the second half of 1993 and the early part of 1994, the organization was already in a state of some disorder: work that had been commissioned in some areas more than a year previously had yet to be collected. By the middle of the year, the operation had closed down entirely. It is not, however, the economy that is directly the point here. Considered artistically, the influence that Operation Hunger – and a number of similar commercially oriented projects – has brought to bear has been

 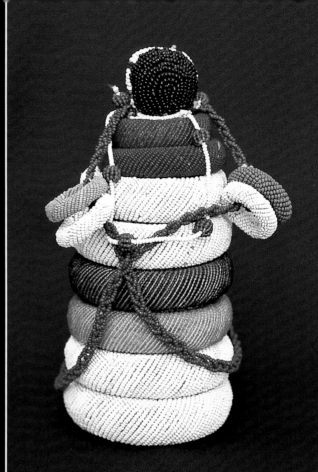

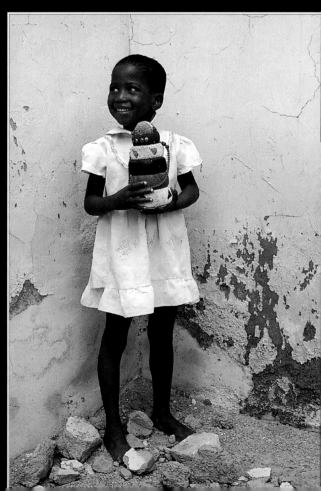

less than salutary. Essentially what it has meant is that the artists of the Ndebele have been turned into mass-producers of beadwork, operating on a quick-turnover basis for a dangerously undiscerning market. Not only has the production of beadwork largely shifted away from its traditional forms towards the making of trinkets with a sufficiently 'African' look to catch the casual tourist's eye, but the production of those items long sanctioned by custom has also been affected.

For the most part the beaded aprons of today are made in a broadly worked geometric style pioneered by Operation Hunger. Usually executed in two or three colours (with golds, greens and blacks predominating) and with no more detail than a simple V-shape and a row of metal beads affixed for punctuation, such pieces can be churned out in the merest fraction of the time it would have taken to produce a piece in any of the earlier Ndebele styles.

It is difficult to take this work seriously in any terms related to the aesthetics of beadworking. Yet even here we should be cautious. Ndebele women themselves have a different, though ambivalent, perception of the new beadworking style. There were many occasions during our field work when, on asking to see the women's beads we would be brought examples of the new 'party style'.

'But don't you have any of the older pieces?' we would ask. 'No,' was the regular reply from the women, and they would then explain that until recently they had possessed examples of the older work but as they were no longer fashionable they had either sold or destroyed them, sometimes recycling the beads for trendy 'new look' creations. More than one woman went so far as to say that if a woman were to wear older beads at contemporary ceremonies, she would be mocked as some kind of anachronism, an old-fashioned old fogey.

But there is another side to the question as well. Speaking to mainly older and certainly more traditionally oriented women, we discovered a surprising fact. More than a few of the women keep hidden – from their peers as much as from would-be buyers and researchers – a special piece of beadwork.

These pieces are used specifically for the purposes of communicating with the ancestors, since, as was explained by more than one informant, 'The ancestors do not recognize the new party-style beads. They only know the old styles.'

## ITEMS OF NDEBELE BEADWORK

In common with many other Nguni tribes, such as the Xhosa and the Zulu, the Ndebele reflect and record the development of the entire life of a woman, from birth through childhood, pubescence, adulthood, marriage, childbearing and to maturity through appropriate forms of beadwork.

### UMUCU

When a child is born, it is equipped with a single strand of beads, known as an *umucu*. At least this is the case in the more traditional framework; the practice appears to have lapsed to a significant extent in recent times. This beaded strand, though not particularly charged with ritual significance, serves as an induction into the tribe and is also supposed to ensure good fortune.

### LIGHABI

Next in the bead cycle (and here it is only girls who are thus equipped) comes the *lighabi*, a leather or canvas loin apron hung with beaded tassels and worn rather like an elaborate fig leaf. It is replaced by larger versions as the young girl grows towards puberty.

### ISIPHEPHETU

Far more elaborate in its working is the *isiphephetu*, a stiff, often somewhat unwieldy, rectangular apron which is

BELOW: *Examples of the 'party-style' beadwork so common at traditional festivities today. More traditionally oriented women assured us that such beadwork is not recognized by the ancestors as being Ndebele.*

LEFT: *Two children wearing* lighabi. *This apron of beaded tassels may be worn by both girls and boys.*

ABOVE: *A woman wearing the metal hoops known as* dzilla *on her legs. The beaded hoops are known as* golwani, *and are also worn in a different version around the neck.*

PAGES 128-129: *Not all Ndebele beadwork has a ritual function. While the stiff beaded* isiphephetu *is traditionally prescribed wear for unmarried girls after initiation, the neck-piece she wears as well as the waistpiece featured on page 128 are mere vanities.*

made and given to the girl by her mother to record the fact that she has undergone the rites of female initiation. The *isiphephetu* is worked with beaded designs; in older versions it was apparently made on stiffened skin, but at least since the early years of the twentieth century, it has been more commonly beaded on a patch of canvas stretched over a piece of board.

By contrast with the *lighabi*, the *isiphephetu's* beading is usually more than merely geometric in its design, and it is here for the first time that the symbolism of the house is essayed in the bead cycle. Often the *isiphephetu* is also the site for more fanciful flights of imagination in Ndebele beading, and such motifs as electric lights, chimneys and telephone poles are often in evidence.

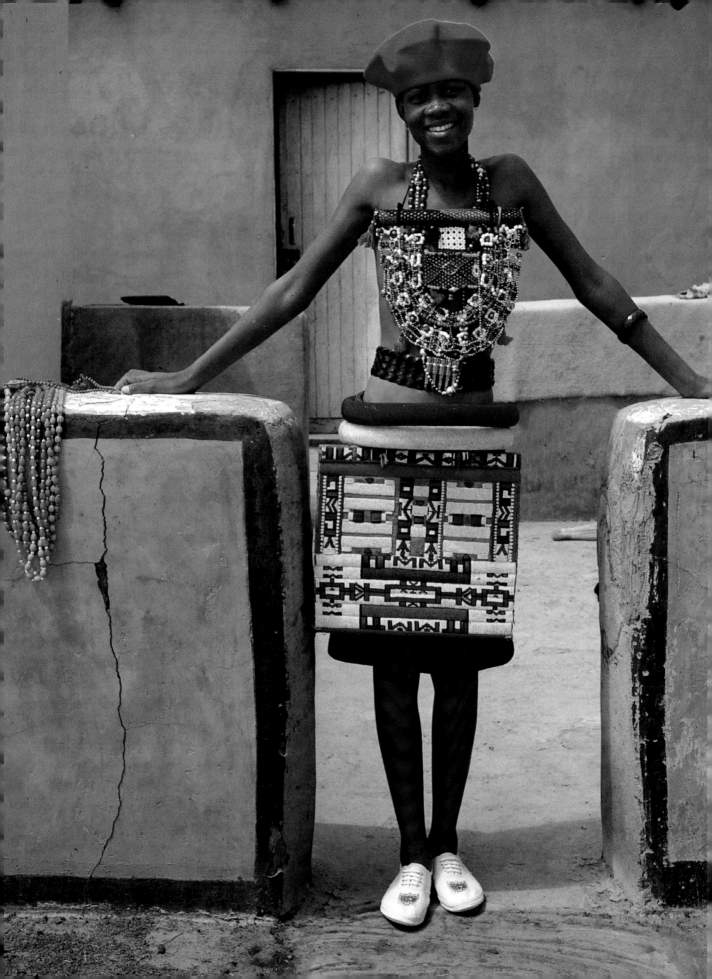

ABOVE AND TOP RIGHT: *Golwani do not usually carry any imagery, but like most items in the traditional Ndebele cannon, they are susceptible to individual nuance. This particularly splendid example, made by Thetiwe Mahlangu of Vleisgewacht in the Nebo district, includes the Ufly or aeroplane motif.*

There is good reason for this: the *isiphephetu* is made by the wearer's mother while the girl is in initiatory seclusion, and it serves to express the mother's aspirations for her daughter. In the older context, these translate themselves into a range of domestic symbolism, mainly in the form of house motifs, but as the bonds of traditional appropriateness have loosened, such motifs as the aeroplane, which in the Ndebele language is known as a 'Ufly', have become increasingly common.

I recall in this regard a particularly fine *isiphephetu* in the 1960s style (though actually made in the 1980s) made by one of many Sophie Mahlangus, this one from Weltevrede. It featured the aeroplane motif and along with this there were electric lights and a runway, designated by the use of black beads with a broken white line running down the middle.

'That is in America,' Sophie Mahlangu explained. 'My daughter, the one who wears this *phephetu*, is inside that Ufly, and she is going to come down in America. This is what I want for my daughter.'

### ISITHIMBA AND AMABEJA

The *isiphephetu* is usually worn together with a backskirt known as an *isithimba*. The latter item is generally made from a semi-circular piece of leather, usually goatskin (though black plastic is often used these days), and sometimes beaded in fairly rudimentary ways. Often the leather of the skirt is suspended from a bead-covered roll of grass, made in much the same way as the *isigolwani*. Finally, a

row of brass rings is often attached, mainly for decorative purposes these days, though some writers believe that in the older context these rings would have served to symbolize wealth.

In earlier times the *isithimba* was often accompanied by a second skirt, known as an *amabeja* and worn over the *isithimba*. Made of a heavy leather band with strings of beads suspended in rows, the *amabeja* provides a kind of curtain, which would come into its own in the dance when the beaded tassels would swing and sweep in such a way as to accentuate the sensuous movements of the hips. This, at least, is what one is able to infer from extant pictures and texts. In all our research in the Ndebele field, however, we did not encounter a single *amabeja* in a situation of use.

Items like the *isithimba* and the *amabeja*, while they do have ritual connotations, are probably best understood in the context of the ceremonies in which they are worn. As noted elsewhere, the ceremonies that mark the conclusion of the female initation, serve at the same time to announce the availability of the recently initiated girls for marriage. The semantics, then, of the apparel worn by the maidens are primarily those of sexual attraction and flirtation. In short, *isithimba* and *amabeja* are, in the Ndebele culture, the equivalent of debutantes' gowns; along with such items as the tambooti necklace and other necklace charms, they are simultaneously vanities and signals to the opposite sex.

### ISIGOLWANI

Equally important in the beautification process are the cumbersome beaded rings known as *izigolwani*. Usually worn in stacks on necks, arms and legs, the *izigolwani* may at some long lost level of memory have been associated with the signification of an appealing fatness, but such meaning is long lost and nowadays they are worn, when they are worn at all, simply as long-sanctioned adornments. Certainly there is no highly charged ritual meaning to them: initiated girls and married women may wear them indiscriminately, but, according to numerous informants, there is no demand on the part of the ancestors that the practice be observed.

*Izigolwani* are made from strips of beads wound around a core of wild grasses. Made to different sizes – some are to be worn around the neck, others around the arms and others again around the legs – they are usually donned in stacks of two, three and more in alternating colours. While the individual rings continue to be monochrome in most cases, since the 1960s some of the larger rings have occasionally carried such designs as the 'Ufly'.

## DZILLA

Though similar in their use to the *izigolwani* – these are also worn on arms and legs as well as around the neck – the brass and copper rings known as *dzilla* have a far more potent traditional identity than the beaded rings. Though only a handful of women still wear them, all of those to whom we spoke who continued the practice of wearing *dzilla*, expressed a powerful belief in their ritual efficacy. The burden of their explanations on the subject was that the wearing of *dzilla* was something ordained by the ancestors and that the wrath of the forefathers would be incurred if these incumbrances were to be removed. Nevertheless, the intensity of such sanctions notwithstanding, the vast majority of Ndebele women have abandoned the wearing of the *dzilla* on a daily basis, and it is one of the curiosities of Ndebele territory that one sees so many necks distended and distorted by the relatively recent wearing of *dzilla* over previously long periods. Many women at least keep up appearances, donning clip-on plastic versions for ceremonial purposes, but as many do not do even this much.

In the traditional framework *dzilla* are reserved for a married woman, and are always given to her by her husband. Traditionally they are beaten from brass or copper rods into a circular shape, then closed around the limb as a permanent fixture. Often, although not always, the first and last of a row of *dzilla* are made from copper, the ones between these being made of brass. In the old days the number of *dzilla* that a man was able to provide for his wife was reckoned as a measure of his wealth, but in the contemporary context – particularly with the presence of the clip-on plastic *dzilla* – such symbolism no longer clings.

What does persist, though, among those women who do continue to wear the *dzilla*, is the sense that they are worn as a token of bondedness to their husband. In the first place, women said they wore these shiny shackles to make themselves beautiful for their husbands. But these seemingly burdensome rings are also worn as a token of faithfulness, even by women whose husbands have departed to the ancestor realms – though the event of widowhood marks the only time that a woman is allowed to remove her *dzilla*. For a period of a year after her husband's death, the woman must remove the rings as a token of mourning, so that she will not, as one informant put it, 'be beautiful for other men'.

BELOW AND PAGES 132-133: *Ndebele women wearing the* nguba *or marriage blanket. The examples on pages 131-132 are both in the 1960s style. The beading on the* nguba *featured on page 133 dates to the 1920s. The original blanket base of this item would long since have had to be replaced and the strips sewn on to a new one.*

BOTTOM LEFT: *The* isithimba *(leather back skirt) and* amabeja *or* mayahani *(the beaded curtain) are worn by young girls of marriagable age. In use, they draw attention to the hips and buttocks, one of the major zones of tittilation in the female form.*

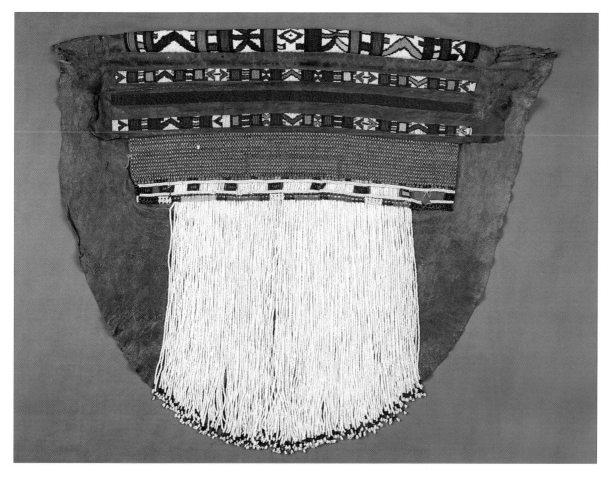

ABOVE: *The apron worn by the model in this picture is the* liphotu. *This is the less formal of the two marriage aprons and in the past would have been worn on everyday occasions. Its symbolism relates to the fact of marriage rather than to the culmination of the marriage in bearing children.*

## LIPHOTU, IJOGOLO AND THE NDEBELE MARRIAGE

Like the *dzilla* the beaded apron, designated as a *liphotu*, is associated with marriage and may not be worn by an unmarried girl. Usually described as an everyday apron, the *liphotu* in fact serves a rather different purpose from the married woman's other beaded apron, the *ijogolo*. The

two different aprons can be traced back to different phases in the extended process of marriage in the Ndebele tradition. This is divided into three different phases, each accompanied by a different ceremony. The first of these phases marks the taking of the woman from her family by the man though before this, complicated negotiations will already have been concluded between the two families, in terms of which a bridal price, or lobola, will have been agreed upon, and a down-payment made. It is at the ceremony to celebrate this first part of the marriage process that the *liphotu* will first be worn by the bride. According to some informants, unlike the beadwork appropriate to younger girls, this is traditionally made by the bride herself during the two-week period of seclusion which she undergoes in preparation for her marriage, though there is little real clarity on this.

The *liphotu* is traditionally made on goatskin, though canvas is not uncommon today. It is distinguished from the *ijogolo* by having two side flaps with beaded tassels hanging in a row between them. Informants confirmed that there was an old symbolism operative here, with the side flaps representing the two marriage partners and the tassels the expectation of the children the woman would bear.

By contrast, the *ijogolo* has five front panels cut from the leather (or canvas) on which the piece is beaded. Again, at least according to researcher, Diane Levy, a fertility symbolism comes into play, with the (often more substantial) middle panel representing the mother and those on either side invoking the children. But in this case it is the *fact* of children and not the expectation. The *ijogolo* marks the culmination of the marriage process, and this, in Ndebele custom, takes place only after the woman has borne children; up until that point she is, so to speak 'on appro', and if she fails to produce children she may be returned and the bridal price refunded. With his wife proven in childbirth, the man must finalize the marriage. He must pay whatever is outstanding on the lobola.

Once this has been done (though in practice the second wedding is often conducted with instalments still outstanding) the third phase of marriage is reached and a final solemnization of the marriage takes place; it is here that the *ijogolo*, made by the women against the event, is ceremonially worn. Thus, in a nutshell, it marks the next step in the progress of the woman through life: though usually described as a marriage apron, it in fact marks the attainment by the woman of the state of motherhood.

## OTHER MARRIAGE BEADWORK

There is a range of other beadwork associated with weddings and with marriage. At the first wedding ceremony, in the traditional framework the bride wears a long beaded train, called an *nyoga* (snake). Made without any backing, simply by weaving beads together, the *nyoga* represents one of the most exquisite and precious of the items of Ndebele beadwork. It is also one of the rarest today, as most weddings are solemnized in Western dress, while the manufacture of the *nyoga* without supporting skin provided scant protection against the ravages of rats and time. Like the marriage beadwork in general, the design of the *nyoga* follows a path from abstract geometricism to basic domestic motif.

Also involved in the traditional wedding ceremony is a cape of beaded goatskin, called a *linaga*, and a veil that covers the woman's face, known as an *isiyaya*. The use of both of these items has significantly lapsed, and nowadays, even in the traditional context, a blanket has supplanted them.

Though there is a good deal more beading that was associated with marriage in the more ceremonial past – both with the ceremony and with the subsequent state of being married – there is only one further item still in use today, and that is the marriage blanket or *nguba*.

Beading is worked on a blanket – usually the colourful so-called Middelburg blanket, with its vertical bands of red, blue, green, yellow and brown, which is given to a woman on the solemnization of her marriage. Although it is just an ordinary blanket to begin with, it frequently develops into an extraordinarily elaborate item as the woman progressively attaches beaded strips to its outer surface, or sometimes works directly on to the fabric of the blanket. Though some informants said the idea was that one strip should be affixed each year, in practice the blankets are decorated (or not) at the woman's discretion.

## LINGA KOBA

Probably the most striking piece of beadwork produced by the Ndebele is the *linga koba* ('long tears'). It records a central event in a woman's life and the wearing of it marks an attainment of status, donned as it is by mothers on the occasion of their sons' return from initiation. Made from two narrow strips of woven beading, one to hang down on each side of the head, and connected by a narrow headband, they are understood to record the woman's simultaneous joy at her son's attainment of manhood and her sorrow at losing her boy. At the same time they mark her own arrival at the next level of maturity.

BOTTOM LEFT: *Along with the* linga koba *and a marriage blanket or* nguba, *the woman in this picture is wearing the five-fingered* ijogolo: *the beaded apron reserved for women who have completed the marriage cycle by bearing children.*

BOTTOM MIDDLE AND BELOW: *Before the wedding ceremony, an Ndebele bride spends a two-week period secluded in a specially made structure inside her parents' home – as shown below. The bride-to-be has to be shielded, particularly from the eyes of men. This explains the use of the umbrella and blanket by the girl in the photograph (middle) – even though her period of seclusion was almost at an end when the picture was taken.*

PAGES 136-137: *A selection of necklaces and the head-dresses known as crowns. Such items are merely festive, not laden with any ritual significance. At top right on page 136 is an example of a tambooti necklace; the carved wooden rectangles of the tambooti are made from a duskily aromatic wood which bears the same name.*

CHAPTER 6

# CONTEMPORARY TRENDS

*Ironically, the distinctive culture of the Ndebele seems more
threatened by liberation and the new society than ever it was by oppression
and apartheid. But there are signs to suggest that it is not so much
dying out as transforming.*

ABOVE AND OPPOSITE: *Details from a mural
representing progress through education at the
gates to a KwaNdebele secondary school in
Pieterskraal.*
PAGE 140: *The façade of the Roman Catholic
Church at Weltevrede, painted by Francina
Ndimande. Francina is an African tradition-
alist; this work was a professional commission.*
PAGE 141: *It is not uncommon to find representational art mixed up with traditional
geometric mural designs – particularly on
business premises – in the former KwaNdebele
homeland. This example was found at a
derelict beer hall in Pieterskraal.*

In the period of transition before South Africa's
first democratic elections in May 1994, sub-
missions were solicited by the multiparty
Negotiating Council for a new South African flag.
Literally hundreds of proposals were put forward. For
the most part they were unremarkable, but what was
remarkable was that nearly all of them looked as if they
had been submitted by Ndebele, or at least by people in
training to become Ndebele. What virtually everyone
had been trying to do was come up with something that
looked distinctively 'African', and, almost automatically,
this had led them to the Ndebele styles.

Nor were the aspirant flag designers the only ones.
The Ndebele look has so completely established itself in
recent years as the quintessentially African look that
people wanting to wear their African credentials on their
sleeves have done so by spontaneously quoting, in one
way or another, the colouful designs associated with the
Ndebele people.

The adoption of the artistic style of the Ndebele is a
curious phenomenon. It is nonetheless more than a passing tribute to the excellence and charm of the work produced within that tribal grouping.

Just as curious is the fact that the only people who
appear to be immune to that charm are the urban
Ndebele; one is far more likely to see Ndebele designs in
the suburbs of traditionally white cities than in the traditionally black townships. Generally speaking, in these
townships there is a noteworthy split in consciousness.

On the one hand traditional ceremonies and observances – such as the customs associated with marriage
and burial – continue to be widely adhered to; sangomas
are regularly consulted by the vast majority of Ndebele
people; and the ancestors continue to be honoured and
to cast their long ancestral shadows in the twilight of
the twentieth century. Yet at the same time the material
culture associated with these traditional practices has all
but disappeared.

The reasons are complex, but not that difficult to
find. For most of this century the notion of ethnicity has
been used by successive white governments to divide the
black majority in South Africa. In the old-style National
Party vision such assertions of tribal separateness would
lead in the end to the recreation of South Africa as a
constellation of separate ethnic states; and, with the
black population thus divided it would easily be ruled.
If such considerations, crudely characterized, under-
wrote the agenda of government, the agenda of liberation politics was aimed at promoting unity and therefore, as often as not, a detribalized self-perception
among black South Africans. The visible expression of
tribal identity became fraught with contradictions; in
the urban context it was often perceived as evidence of
collaboration, and nearly always as anachronistic. The
result was a somewhat ironical situation, with interest
groups associated with the white government of the past
enthusiastically promoting African tradition, and the
inheritors of that tradition rejecting it.

ABOVE: *The birds depicted on the walls are done to a formula for guinea fowl that is frequently used on Ndebele walls. The sales pitch is* sui generis.

It is necessary to understand this because the Ndebele came to figure as one of the prime subjects for the government's exercises in promoting separate ethnic identities. It was the Department of Tourism that was responsible for the creation of the 'tourist village' at KwaMsiza, which in turn served to incubate the art of wallpainting among the Ndebele. It was the interest largely generated in tourist brochures and other publicity exercises from the 1940s onwards that was responsible for creating a trade in the beadwork and other forms of Ndebele material culture and for spawning the relatively numerous books that have been produced on the subject over the years.

The Ndebele should not, however, be seen merely as victims – their culture bought out by the cash that was made available through all this. Rather, what has happened is that the culture has adapted. It has found secret spaces in which to preserve its mysteries, and for the rest it has in many ways flourished under the spotlight – the splendidness of the wallpainting as much as the 1960s style of beadworking bear testimony. In short, the culture has used the situation as much as it has been used within the culture. I am not merely talking in terms of commerce here and the generation of money, though of course this does come into it. I am talking of the more mysterious levels at which cultures shape the identities that provide their representatives with the tools to function in the world.

As argued elsewhere, the art itself has been largely shaped by the peculiarities in its history. However, this is not to say that it lacks authenticity – in fact, just the opposite. What it has reflected is the complex reality of the interface between African and European cultures. This is true from the early years of the twentieth century onwards. For instance, in a good deal of beadwork from the 1930s and later, letters from the Western alphabet have been incorporated into the design of the beadwork. Sometimes such letters are strung together in order to make intelligible words, but just as often they are appropriated merely as geometric designs.

Some informants talked about this as a kind of wish fulfilment, a vicarious ownership of the power of literacy. Many others saw the question more simply: they were reflecting in their art an element of the reality that surrounded them, owning it within the context of the Ndebele tradition.

This is the crucial point: at least until very recent times the tradition has been able to assimilate influences, yet still retain its own identity and its own ways of seeing and using the world. Hence, it has deserved to be looked at as an evolving rather than a decaying tradition. Whether this remains true at the present moment in history is a different question altogether; that a set of traditions has survived oppression provides no guarantee that it will survive freedom.

All the same, it is worth noting here that new signs of adaptation and transformation are already to be discerned among the artists of the Ndebele. New subject matter is continually being essayed, new stylistic devices tried out, and these in the fulness of time may well lead to new developments within the art. In this context, probably the most accomplished of all the Ndebele wall-painters is Francina Ndimande, who in recent painting at her own home has begun to employ a geometricized perspective within her designs. This opening up of the third dimension within the wallpainting brings out a whole new set of possibilities within the ambit of typically Ndebele design, and could conceivably lead to a new flowering.

Such things remain within the realms of the hypothetical. But whether the Ndebele tradition survives or not, the spirit that has long fired the art – one rooted, I have argued, in an impulse towards mediating between African and the Western realities – is to be seen wherever you look in Ndebele country.

At the end of a road that is more boulders than surface, watched by goats in the late afternoon, we come to the home of 'Mr Moses Mahlangu', as it says on a makeshift plaque, and also: 'just keep the gate close please'. Moses Mahlangu's home is an extraordinary place. He has managed to construct a fence almost entirely out of junk: empty soft-drink bottles, old tools

ABOVE: *In recent years Ndebele artists have found a ready market for their work as decoration and consumer items. This radio, decorated by Emmly Masanabo, was featured on a Johannesburg art exhibition in 1993.*

LEFT: *The pride that many Ndebele women take in their stoves is often echoed on the outside walls of their homes. Such motifs appear in abundance – even on houses where cooking in still done in the traditional way, either outdoors or in a specially constructed depression in the floor of the kitchen hut.*

ABOVE: *A business advertisement found on the farm Ongesiens, outside Middelburg.*

and cogs and ratchets and assorted other bits of long-dead machinery, metal signs, scraps of motor cars – and car registration plates (hundreds and hundreds of registration plates).

The effect is bizarre, random, but it is also curiously, itchily beautiful, and when the dying sun catches glints and picks out silhouettes, it looks for a moment like some grand edifice or sculpture. Moses Mahlangu has succeeded in taking the detritus of the white world of the cities and making it into something different, something surprising, something that has a new life and vibrancy.

So too the signage in the rural areas is often strange and extraordinary, positively pulsating with energy and humour and an indefinable sense of revelation. Here is the legend of a sign drawn on an old piece of tin at one of the houses on the farm Ongesiens in the Middelburg district:

STAR SALON
Uma Ufuna Izinwele Ezinhie woza Ubonane no:
Bra: Ace Manje – Reside on special styl
He turn your hair to the style here at Japhtacurl Salon
We've got gel & spray first come first save
Residence at LasVegast

This redefinition of things is something to be seen in the most unexpected places throughout Ndebele territory. A part of the sprawling village of Waterval B in KwaNdebele springs to mind.

Here is every evidence of a forced removal: no houses, only shacks that have been built and extended over the years. It could be a depressing vista, but somehow it is not. A number of shacks have been made into objects of some beauty by the cunning application of different colours of paint on individual sheets of corrugated iron, transforming the walls into a kind of patchwork. There is one in particular that stands out and seems to encapsulate something important. It is a rudimentary affair, made of very basic sheets of zinc and has rocks holding down the roof. But where reality has failed, imagination has taken over: the tin has been painted a powder blue; windows and a door are picked out in red, and a piece of twisted wire draws a television aerial against the sky. It is a lot more moving as a symbol than most monuments. And it might have been an appropriate place at which to end this book, but there is another image with a tale to tell.

In the months we spent in Ndebele territory, we visited the king's kraal at Weltevrede on a number of occasions, but there are two that remain fixed in the mind. On the first, we wait for hours under the spreading marula tree where African court is held. The king meanwhile is on the other side of the retaining wall, busy with whatever keeps kings busy in the mornings. I fall into bizarre conversation with Mjanyelwa Ndimande-Mtsweni, the king's *nyanga*, whom I am meeting for the first time; he explains the provenance of his python-spine necklace, the weird atavistic hunt that has procured the lion's claw, the crocodile's tooth, the underwater death and rebirth which have vouchsafed him his mystical powers. My companions in the meantime are

LEFT AND BOTTOM LEFT: *New uses for old junk at a home in the Bundu Inn area.*
BELOW: *Integrating the forms and materials of the New World. An Ndebele dancing mace incorporates bicycle reflectors and emergency vehicle light-fittings.*
PAGES 146-147: *Urban forms in a rural context: some contemporary Ndebele signage. The house on page 147 (top left) is of particular interest because of the way in which it represents a house on a shack. Though the method is very different, it continues in an imaginative way the traditions of domestic imagery in more familiar forms of Ndebele wallpainting.*

inventing a game of *boules,* using marula fruit, to while away the hours, and some of the men waiting under the tree are beginning to join in. Suddenly the company stiffens. The king is about to make his entrance.

At the back of the complex of buildings inside the perimeter of the homestead, a car starts up. Moments later a wine-red 5-series BMW sweeps around the corner. It is the king; he has made his triumphal progress in the modern Ndebele style, and he is dressed in a suit and much chunky gold jewellery.

When he speaks to his assembled subjects and the visitors from the other side, it is with the voice of an urbane businessman and politician. At length, a flunkey appears, carrying, like ritual objects, a pair of Gucci-style black slip-on shoes, almost exactly like the ones that King Cornelius II already has on his feet. The flunkey goes down on his knees, while the king continues his audience, regally aloof; almost tenderly, and in hieratic submission the flunkey changes the king's shoes. After a while the audience is over, and the king gets back into the ceremonial BMW and roars off in a cloud of dust – to the next of his five houses in the village of Weltevrede. On our next visit the king is not there but more than a hundred men are, and there is a distinct tension in the air. At length we discover what it is about. The assembled dignitaries are the representatives of three Ndebele clans: the Msizas, the Mtswenis and the Ndalas. The reason for their presence is that a prophetess has emerged with what she claims is an important message from the ancestors: that at some point in the ancestral past Mtsweni and Ndala were the sons of Msiza and now the ancestors are demanding that the clans be reunited under the primacy of the Msizas. At least in their dealings with the forefathers, Ndalas and Mtswenis are henceforth to be addressed as 'Msiza', as though that were their given surname. There is much debate and it grows increasingly heated until at length there is a stirring at the gates. A man enters the kraal, staggering and stumbling and wailing. Utterly incoherent, possessed and foaming at the mouth, he proceeds to throw what we would call a fit in the middle of the circle, then he collapses on the ground in a tangled and unconscious heap. It transpires that he is an Ndala, and this is how he responds to this hostile takeover of his identity and to being addressed as Msiza.

We have been reminded that the other hostile takeover – that of African values and custom by those of the West – is far from complete.

FROM THE SMIRNOFF POINT OF VIEW, A CITY HAS TO HAVE A TOUCH OF COLOUR.

SMIRNOFF
PURE SMIRNOFF
WAY DIFFERENT

# GLOSSARY

## A

### ABAKWETHA
Literally 'chosen ones'; the name given to youths undergoing the three-month ordeal of male initiation in Ndebele society.

### AMABEJA/MAYAHANI
An item of beadwork worn by young, unmarried girls after they have completed their period of seclusion which constitutes initiation. It comprises a heavy leather band from which strings of beads are suspended to create a kind of curtain. It is generally worn together with the *isithimba*, a leather backskirt. Drawing attention to the hips and buttocks – traditionally the primary zone of erotic titillation in African societies – the *amabeja* signals availability for marriage. However, it is essentially a decorative rather than ritually charged item of beadwork.

### AMANDLOZI
The tribal ancestors of the Ndebele. Revered and feared by the living, the ancestors are believed to exist in a spirit world which intersects routinely with the world of the living. The tribal ancestors function primarily as guides and guardians of the living, communicating in dreams and through the medium of sangomas.

## B

### BANTU
Though tainted during the apartheid era by its use to designate black people in general, this word simply means 'people'. Strictly, it refers to the group of languages spoken by the majority of peoples inhabiting central and southern Africa. Originating in an area around present-day Nigeria and Cameroon, the earliest Bantu-speakers began to spread through the continent some 3 000 years ago. By the first century AD a branch of the original stock had moved as far as present-day Kenya. From here another long migration saw Bantu-speakers settling in Zimbabwe and South Africa by the third or fourth century AD. Among these were the tribes we today identify as the South Nguni – Zulus, Swazi, Ndebele, Matabele and Xhosas. At the same time, another group had moved southwards to settle in Angola and Zambia, giving rise to, among others, the Sotho-Tswana subgroup of the Bantu. Together these two strains, the South-Nguni and Sotho-Tswana, gave rise to the tribes which comprise the bulk of the black population in South Africa today.

*Dzilla (below and bottom right)*

## D

### DIFAQANE/MFECANE
Literally meaning 'scattering of the people', these terms refer to the great upheavals and migrations of people in southern African during the early 19th century, when – according to the orthodox view at least – Zulu aggression left whole regions depopulated and wasted. As a result of the disruption, new societal formations emerged, with stragglers banding together to form new nations. The word 'mfecane' is the Zulu translation of the Sotho 'difaqane'; which of the two is the more appropriate has been the subject of heated debate among academics in recent years. However, it is worth recording that the whole notion of the 'difaqane/mfecane' has been challenged recently; the argument is based on the belief that the white colonists were at least as guilty of the 'scattering of the people' as were the Zulu warlords.

### DZILLA/IDZILLA
The metal neck, arm and leg rings traditionally worn by married Ndebele women and made for them by their husbands. Characteristically, a series of brass rings is sandwiched between two copper rings on either side. In times gone by the number of rings worn gave an indication of the wealth and status of the wearer.

## G

### GOGO
Grandmother. In Ndebele society – in common with most African societies – the grandmother is treated with great reverence and respect. Among other special functions, the *gogo* rules the homestead.

### GOLWANI/ISIGOLWANI
The thick beaded hoops worn by Ndebele women as decoration, particularly on ceremonial occasions. *Golwani* are wound around grass circlets and, like *dzilla*, are worn as neckpieces and as arm and leg bands. In particular, *golwani* are associated with the costumes worn by marriageable girls at the conclusion of their initiation.

*Golwani*

## I

### IJOGOLO/JOGOLO/JOCOLO/TSHOGOLO
A beaded apron worn by a married woman to celebrate her success in having borne children. Traditionally, the *ijogolo* is one of the most exuberantly decorated and formal of the pieces in an Ndebele woman's bead collection. It usually terminates in five (sometimes four) separate panels which, according to some Ndebele women, represent the children of the union.

*Ijogolo*

### IPORIYANA
Breastplates of animal hide worn by men who have undergone the ordeals of male initiation. Although sometimes beaded in a desultory way, their primary function is totemic. A scrap of hide is affixed to the breastplate (usually made of jackal skin), and symbolizes the clan to which the wearer is affiliated. For instance, a man belonging to the Mtsweni clan – whose totem animal is the baboon and who therefore observes stringent taboos in relation to that animal – will never wear baboon hide, but more probably a scrap of hyaena hide.

### ISANUSI/SANUSI
A select group of 'supersangomas' – witch-doctors – who have undergone the ritual mysteries of death and rebirth. Within the Nguni belief system, the process of becoming *isanusi* requires the individual to spend a protracted period of time under water during which the various denizens of the deep are conquered. Returning to the world of people, the *isanusi* is believed to have conquered death and to have gained privileged access to the truths of the spirit world.

### ISIFISO
Meaning 'wishes', these are the little beaded gourds, bottles, horns and calabashes worn by sangomas on their necklaces. These items are filled with herbal preparations and/or animal extracts, and serve to protect the wearer and signal his or her powers.

### ISIPHEPHETU/PHEPETU

A stiff, rectangular beaded apron worn by young girls after they have completed the period of seclusion which constitutes female initiation. This item is traditionally made by each girl's mother and, reportedly, serves to express the mother's aspirations for her daughter. Thus, most of the symbolism is usually domestic in character.

### ISITHIMBA

A semi-circular backskirt worn on ceremonial occasions by girls of marriageable age. It is traditionally made from goatskin (though plastic is often used these days) and is suspended from a beaded hoop wound around a core of grass. It is sometimes decoratively beaded and often ornamented further with rows of brass rings.

### ISIYAYA

A veil, made from a collection of strung beads and traditionally worn by the bride at the wedding ceremony. Western influences have brought about the less and less frequent use of the *isiyaya* at the wedding ceremony.

*Isiphephetu*

### L LIGHABI/GABI

An apron of beaded tassels hung from a rectangle of leather or canvas. It is usually worn by prepubescent girls, though occasionally small boys are equipped with *lighabi* as well. As the girl grows, so the *lighabi* is replaced by larger versions, and is finally discarded after female initiation.

### LINAGA

A beaded goatskin cape first worn by a woman at the solemnization of her marriage and thereafter at ceremonial occasions. Much prized in the past, *linagas* are relatively rare today.

### LINGA KOBA

Literally 'long tears', these twin beaded strips, often two and three metres long, are worn by matrons whose sons have undergone the ordeals of initiation. Connected by means of a headband, the narrow strips hang on either side of the face, and symbolize the mother's mixed feelings at this time: her joy at her son's attainment of manhood and her sorrow at losing the child. Though subsequently worn routinely at ceremonial occasions, *linga koba* are first donned at the feasts which mark the return of the new men from the *wela*.

### LIPHOTU/MAPOTO/MPOTO

This is one of the key pieces of beadwork associated with marriage. A beaded apron, traditionally made on a goatskin base but today more commonly on canvas, the *liphotu* is first worn by the bride at the wedding ceremony. Usually highly figured, this item is physically distinguished from the married woman's other apron – the *ijogolo* – by the number of panels featured at the bottom extremity of the apron. The *liphotu* includes two panels which are separated by a row of tassels, as opposed to the four or five panels of the *ijogolo*. The two aprons are

*Unbeaded linaga and isiyaya (left); beaded linaga (right)*

symbolically distinct: the tassels of the *liphotu* reportedly represent the expectation of children, while the *ijogolo* is worn only after the woman has borne children to celebrate this fact.

### LOBOLA

The price paid in very many African societies by a man (or his family) to secure the hand of a girl or woman in marriage. Traditionally lobola is paid in livestock, though through Western influence cash payments are now at least as common. The wedding usually takes place after a portion of the total lobola has been paid. Lobola or part thereof is sometimes refundable if the woman fails to produce children.

### M MANALA (SEE ALSO NDZUNDZA)

One of the two major subgroups of the southern Ndebele people. The division into two branches

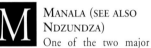

*Linga koba*

probably occurred around the end of the 18th century, reflecting a battle for succession between two brothers, Manala and Ndzundza. The Manala never consolidated – unlike the Ndzundza – after the devastation and dispersal caused by the difaqane, and by the early decades of the 20th century, were largely represented by a band of survivors gathered around a mission station at Wallmansthal, outside Pretoria. In the 1980s, after the establishment of the KwaNdebele homeland, an (unsuccessful) attempt was launched by the apartheid government to oust the Ndzundza royal lineage from the territory and instate the Manala chieftaincy in its stead.

Although the artistic styles adopted by the Manala are barely distinguishable from those of the Ndzundza, the great flowering of artistic expression among the Ndebele in the 20th century took place primarily among the Ndzundza.

### MATABELE

Sometimes, and confusingly, also referred to as Ndebele or northern Ndebele, these are in fact the descendants of the Zulu warlord, Mzilikazi, and his impis, and represent a far later migration of the Nguni than do the southern Ndebele. Shaka's half-brother and rival, Mzilikazi was one of the major agents of the difaqane, and, after cutting a swathe through the subcontinent, he and his followers eventually settled in present-day Zimbabwe.

## MPHANDU

A makeshift shelter in which male initiates are housed during the *wela*. It is built for the initiates by their older brothers who also serve as their guides and protectors during the ordeal.

## MTUNZI

A usually shaded enclosure attached to the Ndebele homestead, and reserved for use by men. Traditionally, it is located outside the enclosing walls of the homestead and near the cattle byre.

## N NDAU

An Nguni people living in central Mozambique and Zimbabwe. The tradition of Nguni divination which involves the witch-doctor's bones is associated with the Ndau and also bears their name.

## NDEBELE /AMANDEBELE/ SOUTH NDEBELE

A south Nguni people who by the 16th century had emerged as a separate group and were settled in the eastern parts of the Transvaal Province of South Africa. The Ndebele are divided into the Ndzundza and the Manala subgroups, and during apartheid rule and its notorious 'bantustans' policy were allocated approximately 50 000 hectares of land around the royal seat of Weltevrede as the KwaNdebele ethnic 'homeland'.

## NDZUNDZA

The major branch of the Ndebele and the group primarily responsible for the art and culture dealt with in this book. Emerging as a major regional power in the middle years of the 19th century, the Ndzundza were finally defeated by the Boers of the Transvaal Republic. This came about after a long siege of the Ndzundza stronghold at Mapoch's Caves (also known as KoNomtjharhelo) in 1883, and saw the Ndzundza subjected to a five year period as indentured labourers. It was notably among the Ndzundza, rather than the Manala, that the cultural institutions generally regarded as definitive of Ndebele culture were maintained and developed.

*Nyoga*

*Nguba*

## NGUBA

The marriage blanket worn by Ndebele women. Usually made from the so-called Middelburg blanket – a commercially available blanket patterned with vertical stripes of green, red, blue, yellow and brown – it is customized with beadwork by the owner. It often becomes a spectacular and elaborate item as the woman continues to add strips of beading throughout the course of

*Nguba*

*The nyanga Mjanyelwa Naimandi-Mtsweni*

her marriage. In the past women were required to wear their marriage blankets whenever they appeared in public, but nowadays any blanket or stole suffices.

## NGUNI

A subgroup of Bantu languages of southern Africa, including Zulu, Xhosa, Swazi and Ndebele. All belong to the southern branch of the Nguni people, sharing many customs as well as linguistic characteristics. The word 'Nguni' also designates the herbal (as opposed to divinatory) practices of the Ndebele as used in traditional medicine.

## NYANGA

A healer who exclusively practises the Nguni traditions of herbal medicine. Unlike the sangoma, the *nyanga* does not receive his vocation via an initiatory illness, but studies under an experienced practitioner. Nevertheless, there is a mystical element to the practice of the *nyanga*: many claim that their learning, in part at least, is handed over by guardian ancestors in dreams.

## NYOGA

Translating as 'snake', the *nyoga* is a long beaded train, often more than a metre in length, and is worn as part of the bridal costume. Though seldom in use today, the *nyoga* is made solely of beads and takes many months to make. The older examples, particularly, are highly prized by collectors.

## P PLASTICI

During the 1960s and 1970s plastic was widely used in the making of marriage aprons and other pieces of ceremonial dress. With brightly coloured plastic trim and imaginative figuration, such '*plastici*' began to emerge as something of an art form. However, as the production of Ndebele artefacts has become increasingly market-oriented (collectors tending to scorn such productions as 'unauthentic') *plastici* have declined markedly. Today, where they are used at all, they tend to be sorry and disposable items, made of rubbish bags with usually shoddily applied insulation tape.

*Plastici*

## POMET

Also known as a 'Driver's Licence' or a 'Code 10 Driver's Licence', this is traditionally a piece of beadwork (although these days it can also be an embroidered 'certificate') which serves to establish that the bearer is a matron of standing within the traditional life of the Ndebele. The bearer of the pomet is responsible for the maintenance of traditional observances at ceremonial functions.

## SANGOMA

The word 'sangoma' literally means 'people of the drum'. The sangoma is essentially a shamanistic healer whose connection with the world of the spirits gives him/her both special status and special powers within Ndebele (and, generally, African) society. Called through some kind of illness – usually what we might term 'madness' – to their vocation, sangomas are guided by the spirit of one of more ancestors, though also serve an apprenticeship with an experienced sangoma. Initiated into the path of sangomahood through a ritual sacrifice, these traditional healers – in common with shamans around the world – use drums and ecstatic dancing to achieve visionary and trance states. Sangomas practise divinatory techniques using bones as a healing method and also use the herbal preparations proper to *nyangas*.

*Stitirimba (visible between legs)*

### SHAMAN

A 'wounded healer'; the figure of the shaman is found with remarkable consistency among hunter-gatherer and animal-husbanding societies around the world. Among the features of the shaman's identity as a healer are: the illness through which he/she is believed to gain access to the world of the dead; the use of the drum and of dancing as a means to ecstasy and spiritual vision; and the use of intoxicants as aids to enlightenment.

### SONYANA

A grass headband worn by boys when they leave home to embark on the three-month period of male initiation or *wela*.

### SOTHO-TSWANA

One of the southern African language groups. Like the Nguni, the Sotho-Tswana are of Bantu origin; their migration, however, was primarily down the west coast of Africa, whereas the Nguni migration took place southwards from present-day Kenya.

*Nyoga*

### STITIRIMBA

A strip of animal hide worn rather like a tail by men who have completed the rites of initiation. It is first worn by a youth on his return from the *wela*, and traditionally is made by his grandfather in anticipation of the youth's ascent to manhood.

## TAMBOOTI

A necklace made usually of carved squares of the wood which carry the same name. It is most commonly worn by girls at parties celebrating the female initiation. More flirtatious than of any ritual significance, tambootis are particularly prized because of their rich musky smell which derives from the wood.

*'Ufly'*

## UMUCU

A simple string of beads worn around the waist as a kind of charm by infants and young children of both sexes.

### UFLY

The aeroplane motif found since the 1960s in Ndebele wallpainting and beadwork.

## WELA/INGOMA

The three-month initiation process of Ndebele males. Proceeding with ritual circumcision, it is followed by a period during which the youths live isolated – except from their older brothers and specially appointed elders – in the bush. The experience is as much an ordeal as an introduction to the lore of the tribe. Returning from the *wela*, the youths are considered to be men and full members of the tribe.

*Isigolwani with 'Ufly'*

# INDEX

Numbers in **bold** type refer to the main sections of text; *italic* type denotes photographic references

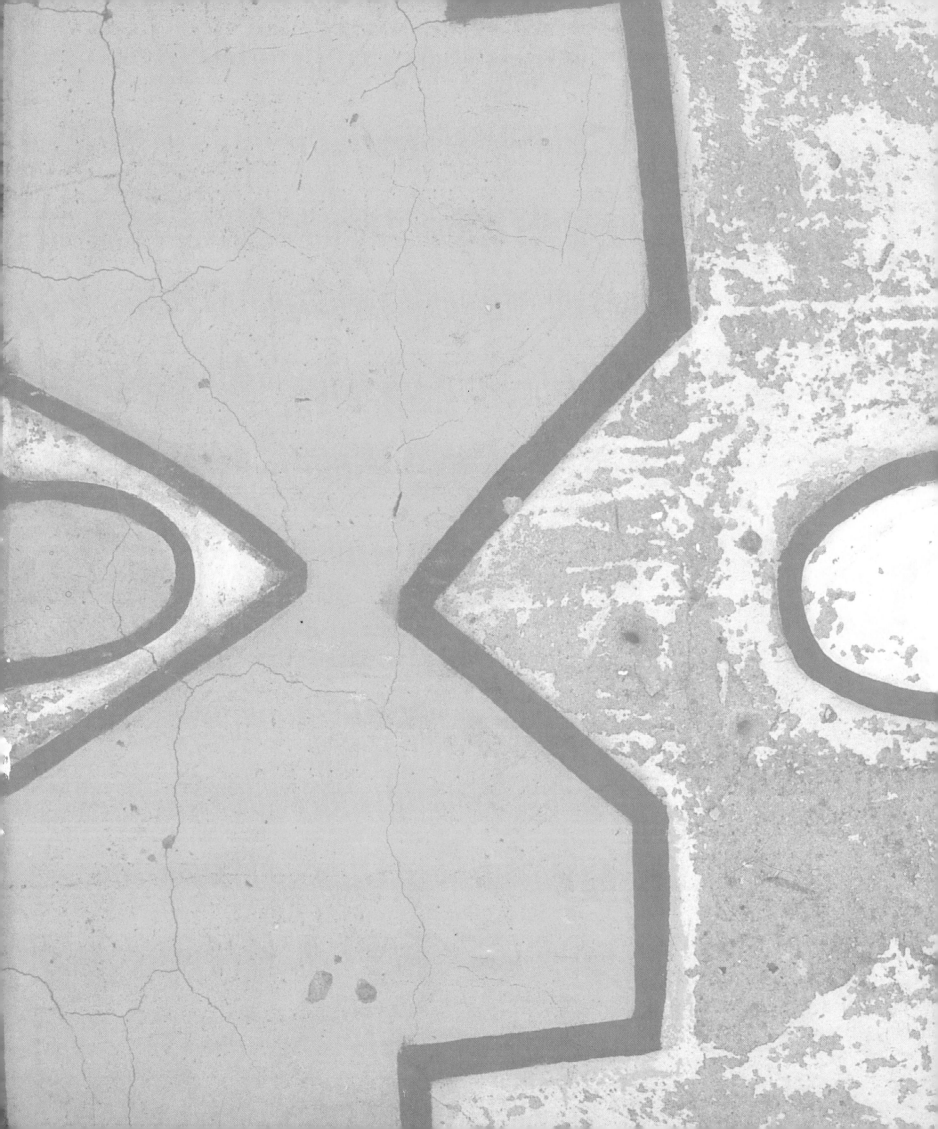